MICROSOFT®
EXCEL 2000

BRIEF EDITION

ADVANTAGE

SERIES

MICROSOFT®

EXCEL 2000

BRIEF EDITION

Sarah E. Hutchinson

Glen J. Coulthard

Information Technology

McGraw-Hill
Irwin

Boston   Burr Ridge, IL   Dubuque, IA   Madison, WI   New York   San Francisco   St. Louis
Bangkok   Bogotá   Caracas   Kuala Lumpur   Lisbon   London   Madrid   Mexico City
Milan   Montreal   New Delhi   Santiago   Seoul   Singapore   Sydney   Taipei   Toronto

McGraw-Hill Higher Education

A Division of The **McGraw-Hill** *Companies*

MICROSOFT® EXCEL 2000 BRIEF EDITION

3 4 5 6 7 8 9 0 WEB/WEB 9 0 9 8 7 6 5 4 3 2 1

ISBN 0-07-233796-6

Director & publisher: *David Brake*

Sponsoring editor: *Trisha O'Shea*

Developmental editor: *Kyle Thomes*

Senior marketing manager: *Jodi McPherson*

Project manager: *Christina Thornton-Villagomez*

Production supervisor: *Debra R. Benson*

Designer: *A.M. Design*

Compositor: *GTS Graphics*

Typeface: *11/13 Stone Serif*

Printer: *Webcrafters, Inc.*

Library of Congress Cataloging-in-Publication Data

Hutchinson, Sarah E.
    Microsoft Excel 2000 : brief edition / Sarah E. Hutchinson, Glen J. Coulthard.
      p. cm. Advantage series for computer education
    ISBN 0-07-233796-6 (softcover : alk. paper)
    Includes index.
    1. Microsoft Excel (Computer file).   I. Coulthard, Glen J.   II. Title.
III. Series
HF5548.4.M523H868   2000
005.369 dc—21   99-12479

http://www.mhhe.com

InformationTechnology

Preface The Advantage Series

Goals/Philosophy

The Advantage Series presents the **What, Why, and How** of computer application skills to today's students. Each lab manual is built upon an efficient learning model, which provides students and faculty with complete coverage of the most powerful software packages available today.

Approach

The Advantage Series builds upon an efficient learning model, which provides students and faculty with complete coverage and enhances critical thinking skills. This case-based, "problem-solving" approach teaches the What, Why, and How of computer application skills.

The Advantage Series introduces the **"Feature-Method-Practice"** layered approach. The **Feature** describes the command and tells the importance of that command. The **Method** shows students how to perform the Feature. The **Practice** allows students to apply the feature in a keystroke exercise.

About the Series

The Advantage Series offers *three levels* of instruction. Each level builds upon the previous level. The following are the three level of instructions:

Brief: covers the basics of the application, contains two to four chapters, and is typically 120–190 pages long.

Introductory: includes the material in the Brief Lab manual plus two to three additional chapters. The Introductory lab manuals are approximately 300 pages long and prepare students for the *Microsoft Office User Specialist Proficient Exam (MOUS Certification)*

Complete: includes the Introductory lab manual plus an additional five chapters of advanced level content. The Complete lab manuals are approximately 600 pages in length and prepare students to take the *Microsoft Office User Specialist Expert Exam (MOUS Certification)*.

EXCEL

About the Book

Each Lab manual features the following:

- **Learning Objectives:** At the beginning of each chapter, a list of action-oriented objectives is presented detailing what is expected of the students.

- **Chapters:** Each lab manual is divided into chapters.

- **Modules:** Each chapter contains three to five independent modules, requiring approximately 30–45 minutes each to complete. Although we recommend you complete an entire chapter before proceeding, you may skip or rearrange the order of these modules to best suit your learning needs.

Case Study

- **Case Studies:** Each chapter, begins with a Case Study. The student is introduced to a fictitious person or company and their immediate problem or opportunity. Throughout the chapter students obtain the knowledge and skills necessary to meet the challenges presented in the Case Study. At the end of each chapter, students are asked to solve problems directly related to the Case Study.

- **Feature-Method-Practice:** Each chapter highlights our **unique "Feature-Method-Practice"** layered approach. The **Feature** layer describes the command or technique and persuades you of its importance and relevance. The **Method** layer shows you how to perform the procedure, while the **Practice** layer lets you apply the feature in a hands-on step-by-step exercise.

- **Instructions:** The numbered step-by-step progression for all hands on examples and exercises are clearly identified. Students will find it surprisingly easy to follow the logical sequence of keystrokes and mouse clicks, and no longer worry about missing a step.

In Addition

- **In Addition Boxes:** These content boxes are placed strategically throughout the chapter and provide information on advanced topics that are beyond the scope of the current discussion.

- **Self Check Boxes:** At the end of each module, a brief self-check question appears for students to test their comprehension of the material. Answers for these questions appear in the Appendix.

- **Chapter Review:** The *Command Summary* and *Key Terms* provide an excellent review of the chapter content and prepare students for the short-answer, true-false and multiple-choice questions at the end of each chapter.

Easy ●
Moderate ■
Difficult ◆

- **Hands-On Projects:** Each chapter concludes with six hands-on projects that are rated according to their difficulty level. The *easy* and *moderate* projects use a running-case approach, whereby the same person or company appears at the end of each chapter in a particular tutorial. The two *difficult* or *on your own* projects provide greater latitude in applying the software to a variety of creative problem-solving situations.

- **Appendix: Microsoft Windows Quick Reference:** Each lab manual contains a Microsoft Windows Quick Reference. This Quick reference teaches students the fundamentals of using a mouse and a keyboard, illustrates how to interact with a Dialogue box, and describes the fundamentals of how to use the Office 2000 Help System.

Instructions: The numbered step-by-step progression for all hands-on examples and exercises are clearly identified. Students will find it surprisingly easy to follow the logical sequence of keystrokes and mouse clicks, and no longer worry about missing a step.

8 To return to a multicolumn list format:
CLICK: down arrow beside the Views button
CHOOSE: List

9 Let's open one of the documents in the list area:
DOUBLE-CLICK: WRD140
The dialog box disappears and the document is loaded into the application window. (*Note:* The "WRD140" filename reflects that this document is used in module 1.4 of the Word learning guide.)

10 Close the document before proceeding.

In Addition Boxes: These content boxes are placed strategically throughout the chapter and provide information on advanced topics that are beyond the scope of the current discussion.

In Addition
Storing and Retrieving Files on Web Servers

With the appropriate network connection, you can open and save Word documents on the Internet. In the Open or Save As dialog boxes, click the Web Folders button () in the Places bar or select an FTP Internet site from the *Look in* drop-down list. This feature allows you to share and update Word documents with users from around the world.

Self Check Boxes: At the end of each module, a brief self-check question appears for students to test their comprehension of the material. Answers for these questions appear in the Appendix.

1.4 Self Check In the Open and Save As dialog boxes, how do the List and Details views differ?

1.5 Previewing and Printing

This module focuses on outputting your document creations. Most commonly, you will print a document for inclusion into a report or other such document.

1.5.1 Previewing a Document

Feature-Method-Practice: Each chapter highlights our unique "Feature-Method-Practice" layered approach. The *Feature* layer describes the command or technique and persuades you of its importance and relevance. The *Method* layer shows you how to perform the procedure, while the *Practice* layer lets you apply the feature in a hands-on step-by-step exercise.

FEATURE
Before sending a document to the printer, you can preview it using a full-page display that closely resembles the printed version. In this Preview display mode, you can move through the document pages, and zoom in and out on desired areas.

METHOD
CLICK: Print Preview button (🔍), or
CHOOSE: File, Print Preview

PRACTICE
You will now open a relatively large document and then preview it on the screen.

Case Studies: Each chapter, begins with a Case Study. Throughout the chapter students obtain the knowledge and skills necessary to meet the challenges presented in the Case Study. At the end of each chapter, students are asked to solve problems directly related to the Case Study.

Case Study

1-on-1 Tutoring Services

Dean Shearwater is helping to pay his university tuition by tutoring other university and high school students. Over the last two years, he has developed an excellent reputation for making complex topics simple and easy to remember. While he is an excellent tutor, last year he didn't earn as much as he had expected.

Dean thinks his lackluster earnings can be attributed to poor advertising and inadequate record keeping. This year, he has decided to operate his tutoring services more like a real business. His first priority is to learn how to use Microsoft Word so that he can prepare advertising materials, send faxes and memos, and organize his student notes.

In this chapter, you and Dean learn how to create simple documents from scratch, use built-in document templates, edit documents, and use the Undo command. You also learn how to preview and print your work.

Chapters: Each lab manual is divided into chapters. Each chapter is composed of 2–5 *Modules.* Each module is composed of one or more *Lessons.*

1.1 Getting Started with Word

Microsoft Word 2000 is a **word processing** program that enables you to create, edit, format, and print many types of documents including résumés and cover letters, reports and proposals, World Wide Web pages, and more. By the time you complete this learning guide, you will be skilled in creating all types of documents and in getting them to look the way you want. In this module, you load Microsoft Word and proceed through a guided tour of its primary components.

1.1.1 Loading and Exiting Word

New Design: The *new* Advantage Series design offers a shaded area where the Featured-Method-Practice and numbered step-by-step instructions maintain the focus of the student.

FEATURE
You load Word from the Windows Start menu, accessed by clicking the Start button (Start) on the taskbar. Because Word requires a significant amount of memory, you should always exit the application when you are finished doing your work. Most Windows applications allow you to close their windows by clicking the Close button (x) appearing in the top right-hand corner.

Teaching Resources

The following is a list of supplemental material, which can be used to teach this course.

ATLAS

ATLAS—Active Testing and Learning Assessment Software— available for The *Advantage Series* is our cutting edge "Real Time Assessment" software. It's not what you do, it's how you do it. Students perform task while working live within the office applications environment. ATLAS can be delivered three ways: over a network, on a stand alone PC, or via the Web. Atlas will offer complete customization with flexibility to create and design course content.

Instructor's Resource Kits

The Instructors Resource Kit provides professors with all of the ancillary material needed to teach a course. Irwin/McGraw-Hill is committed to providing instructors with the most effective instructional resources available. Many of these resources are available at our **Information Technology Supersite** *www.mhhe.com/it.* Our Instructor's Resource Kits are available on CD-ROM and contain the following:

- **Diploma by Brownstone**—is the most flexible, powerful, and easy to use computerized testing system available in higher education. The diploma system allows professors to create an exam as a printed version, as a LAN-based Online version and as an Internet version. Diploma includes grade book features, which automate the entire testing process.

- **Instructor's Manual**—Includes:
  —Solutions to all lessons and end of chapter material
  —Teaching Tips
  —Teaching Strategies
  —Additional exercises

- **Student Data Files**—To use the Advantage Series students must have Data Files to complete practice and test sessions. The instructor and students using this text in classes are granted the right to post the student files on any network or stand-alone computer, or to distribute the files on individual diskettes. The student files may be downloaded from our IT Supersite at www.mhhe.com/it.

- **Series Web Site**—Available at www.mhhe.com/cit/apps/adv/.

EXCEL

Digital Solutions

PageOut Lite—allows an instructor to create their own basic Web site hosted by McGraw-Hill. PageOut Lite includes three basic templates that automatically convert typed material into html Web Pages. Using PageOut Lite an instructor can set up a homepage, Web links, and a basic course syllabus and lecture notes.

PageOut—is Irwin/McGraw-Hill's Course Webster Development Center. Pageout allows an instructor to create a more complex course Webster with an interactive syllabus and some course management features. Like PageOut Lite, PageOut converts typed material to html. For more information please visit the Pageout Web site at www.mhla.net/pageout.

OLC/Series Web Sites—Online Learning Centers (OLC's)/Series Sites are accessible through our Supersite at www.mhhe.com/it. Our OLC/Series Sites provide pedagogical features and supplements for our titles online. Students can point and click their way to key terms, learning objectives, chapter overviews, PowerPoint slides, exercises and web links.

The McGraw-Hill Learning Architecture (MHLA)—is a complete course delivery system. MHLA gives professors ownership in the way digital content is presented to the class through online quizzing, student collaboration, course administration, and content management. For a walkthrough of MHLA, visit the MHLA Web site at www.mhla.net.

Packaging Options

For more information about our discount options, contact your local Irwin/McGraw-Hill Sales representative at 1-800-338-3987 or visit our Web site at www.mhhe.com/it.

Acknowledgments

This series of tutorials is the direct result of the teamwork and heart of many people. We sincerely thank the reviewers, instructors, and students who have shared their comments and suggestions with us over the past few years. We do read them! With their valuable feedback, our tutorials have evolved into the product you see before you.

Many thanks go to Kyle Lewis, Trisha O'Shea, Kyle Thomes, and Carrie Berkshire from Irwin/McGraw-Hill whose management helped to get this book produced in a timely and efficient manner. Special recognition goes to all of the individuals mentioned in the credits at the beginning of this tutorial. And finally, to the many others who weren't directly involved in this project but who have stood by us the whole way, we appreciate your encouragement and support.

The Advantage Team
Special thanks go out to our contributing members on the Advantage team.

Verlaine Murphy
Walt Musekamp
Ingrid Neumann
Catherine Schuler

Write to Us
We welcome your response to this tutorial, for we are trying to make it as useful a learning tool as possible. Please contact us at

Sarah E. Hutchinson—sclifford@mindspring.com
Glen J. Coulthard—glen@coulthard.com

Contents

CREATING A WORKSHEET

CASE STUDY 5

1.1 GETTING STARTED WITH EXCEL 5
1.1.1 Loading and Exiting Excel, **7**
1.1.2 Touring Excel, **8**
1.1.3 Customizing Menus and Toolbars, **10**

1.2 CREATING YOUR FIRST WORKSHEET 12
1.2.1 Moving the Cell Pointer, **13**
1.2.2 Entering Text, **15**
1.2.3 Entering Dates, **16**
1.2.4 Entering Numbers, **18**
1.2.5 Entering Formulas, **19**

1.3 EDITING YOUR WORK 21
1.3.1 Editing a Cell's Contents, **21**
1.3.2 Erasing a Cell, **23**
1.3.3 Using Undo and Redo, **25**

1.4 MANAGING FILES 27
1.4.1 Beginning a New Workbook, **28**
1.4.2 Saving and Closing, **30**
1.4.3 Opening an Existing Workbook, **32**

1.5 CHAPTER REVIEW 34
1.6 REVIEW QUESTIONS 37
1.7 HANDS-ON PROJECT 40
1.8 CASE PROBLEMS 47

MODIFYING A WORKSHEET   CHAPTER 2

CASE STUDY 53

2.1 ENTERING AND REVIEWING DATA 53
2.1.1 Selecting Cells and Ranges, **53**
2.1.2 Entering Data Using AutoComplete, **56**
2.1.3 Using AutoCalculate and AutoSum, **59**
2.1.4 Inserting and Deleting Cells, **61**

2.2 COPYING AND MOVING DATA 63
2.2.1 Using the Clipboards, **64**
2.2.2 Using Drag and Drop, **68**
2.2.3 Creating a Series Using AutoFill, **70**

2.2.4 Extending a Cell's Contents, **72**

2.3 MODIFYING ROWS AND COLUMNS 74
2.3.1 Changing Column Widths, **74**
2.3.2 Changing Row Heights, **77**
2.3.3 Inserting and Deleting Rows and Columns, **78**
2.3.4 Hiding and Unhiding Rows and Columns, **81**

2.4 CHAPTER REVIEW 83
2.5 REVIEW QUESTIONS 85
2.6 HANDS-ON PROJECTS 88
2.7 CASE PROBLEMS 94

FORMATTING AND PRINTING

CASE STUDY 101

3.1 ENHANCING A WORKSHEET'S APPEARANCE 101

3.1.1 Applying Fonts, Font Styles, and Colors, **102**

3.1.2 Formatting Numbers and Dates, **104**

3.1.3 Aligning and Merging Cells, **107**

3.1.4 Adding Borders and Shading, **110**

3.2 APPLYING AND REMOVING FORMATTING 112

3.2.1 Using Format Painter, **113**

3.2.2 Removing Formatting Attributes, **116**

3.2.3 Using the Paste Special Command, **117**

3.2.4 Using the AutoFormat Command, **119**

3.3 PRINTING AND WEB PUBLISHING 121

3.3.1 Previewing and Printing a Worksheet, **122**

3.3.2 Previewing and Publishing to the Web, **124**

3.4 CUSTOMIZING PRINT OPTIONS 126

3.4.1 Adjusting Page and Margin Settings, **127**

3.4.2 Inserting Headers and Footers, **128**

3.4.3 Selecting Worksheet Content to Print, **130**

3.5 CHAPTER REVIEW 133

3.6 REVIEW QUESTION 135

3.7 HANDS-ON PROJECTS 138

CASE PROBLEMS 145

CASE STUDY 151

4.1 WORKING WITH NAMED RANGES 151

    4.1.1 Naming Cell Ranges, **152**

    4.1.2 Managing Range Names, **155**

    4.1.3 Using References in Formulas, **157**

    4.1.4 Entering Natural Language Formulas, **159**

4.2 USING BUILT-IN FUNCTIONS 163

    4.2.1 Adding Values (SUM), **163**

    4.2.2 Calculating Averages (AVERAGE), **164**

    4.2.3 Counting Values (COUNT), **166**

    4.2.4 Analyzing Values (MIN and MAX), **167**

    4.2.5 Calculating Dates (NOW and TODAY), **169**

4.3 CREATING AN EMBEDDED CHART 173

    4.3.1 Creating a Chart Using the Chart Wizard, **173**

    4.3.2 Previewing and Printing an Embedded Chart, **177**

4.4 CHAPTER REVIEW 179

4.5 REVIEW QUESTIONS 181

4.6 HANDS-ON PROJECTS 184

4.7 CASE PROBLEMS 190

ANSWERS TO SELF CHECK 193

GLOSSARY 195

APPENDIX 199

INDEX 206

MICROSOFT®
EXCEL 2000

BRIEF EDITION

MICROSOFT EXCEL 2000
Creating a Worksheet

CHAPTER

ONE

Chapter Outline

1.1 Getting Started with Excel

1.2 Creating Your First Worksheet

1.3 Editing Your Work

1.4 Managing Files

1.5 Chapter Review

1.6 Review Questions

1.7 Hands-On Projects

1.8 Case Problems

Learning Objectives

After reading this chapter, you will be able to:

- Describe the different components of the application and workbook windows

- Select commands using the Menu bar and right-click menus

- Enter text, dates, numbers, and formulas in a worksheet

- Edit and erase cell data

- Use the Undo and Redo commands

- Start a new workbook

- Save, open, and close a workbook

Case Study

Rain Coast Air

Rain Coast Air is a small, privately owned airline charter company operating in the Pacific Northwest. The company's typical charter business consists of flying tourists to remote fishing lodges and transporting geological and forestry survey crews. Earlier this year, Rain Coast added a third aircraft to their fleet of float planes and retained two full-time and three part-time pilots. Along with the pilots, Rain Coast employs a dock hand and a mechanic. Hank Frobisher, the general manager, started the company and oversees all aspects of its operation.

To date, Rain Coast has been operating with a bare minimum of paperwork and manual record-keeping. All bookings are hand-written into a scheduling chart and the pilots fill out trip logs at the end of each flight. Invoices and receipts are simply turned over to a bookkeeping service as Hank cannot afford a staff accountant. Just lately, however, Hank is finding it increasingly difficult to obtain the information he needs to make key business decisions. To remedy this, he hired Jennifer Duvall, the daughter of one of his pilots, as an office assistant. Jennifer is enrolled in a Microsoft Excel course at the local community college and has expressed some enthusiasm in setting up worksheets for Rain Coast Air.

In this chapter, you and Jennifer learn how to work with Microsoft Excel. Specifically, you create new worksheets from scratch and enter text, numbers, dates, and formulas. Then you learn how to edit and modify cell entries and even practice using the Undo command. To complete the chapter, you practice saving and opening workbooks.

1.1 Getting Started with Excel

Microsoft Excel 2000 is an electronic spreadsheet program that enables you to store, manipulate, and chart numeric data. Researchers, statisticians, and business people use spreadsheet software to analyze and summarize mathematical, statistical, and financial data. Closer to home, you can use Excel to create a budget for your monthly living expenses, analyze returns in the stock market, develop a business plan, or calculate the loan payment required to purchase a new car.

Excel enables you to create and modify worksheets—the electronic version of an accountant's ledger pad—and chart sheets. A **worksheet** (Figure 1.1) is divided into vertical columns and horizontal rows. The rows are numbered and the columns are labeled from A to Z, then AA to AZ, and so on to column IV. The intersection of a column and a row is called a **cell.** Each cell is given a **cell address,** like a post office box number, consisting of its column letter followed by its row number (for example, B4 or FX400). Excel allows you to open multiple worksheets and chart sheets within its application window.

Figure 1.1

An electronic worksheet

	A	B	C	D	E	F	G
1			Mutual Fund Manager				
2							
3	Date	Close	Shares	Value	Volume	High	Low
4	7/31/99	9.98	1420.123	$14,172.83			
5	6/30/99	10.52	1420.123	$14,939.69			
6	5/31/99	10.62	1420.123	$15,081.71			
7	4/30/99	10.15	1420.123	$14,414.25			
8	3/31/99	9.95	511.274	$5,087.18			
9	2/28/99	9.74	511.274	$4,979.81			
10	1/31/99	9.78	511.274	$5,000.26			
11							
12							
13							

Sheet1 / Sheet2 / Sheet3

A **chart sheet** (Figure 1.2) displays a chart graphic that is typically linked to data stored in a worksheet. When the data is changed, the chart is updated automatically to reflect the new information. Charts may also appear alongside their data in a worksheet.

Figure 1.2

A chart sheet

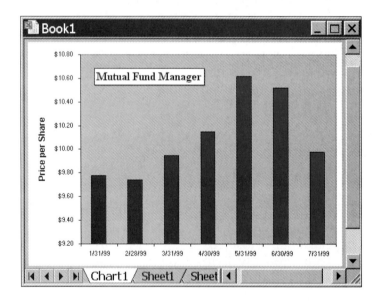

Related worksheets and chart sheets are stored together in a single disk file called a **workbook.** You can think of an Excel workbook as a three-ring binder with tabs at the beginning of each new page or sheet. In this module, you load Microsoft Excel and proceed through a guided tour of its application and document windows.

EXCEL

1.1.1 Loading and Exiting Excel

FEATURE

You load Excel from the Windows Start menu, accessed by clicking the Start button (🏁Start) on the taskbar. Because Excel requires a significant amount of memory, you should always exit the application when you are finished doing your work. Most Windows applications allow you to close their windows by clicking on the Close button (☒) appearing in the top right-hand corner.

METHOD

- To load Excel:
  CLICK: Start button (🏁Start)
  CHOOSE: Programs, Microsoft Excel
- To exit Excel:
  CHOOSE: File, Exit from Excel's Menu bar

PRACTICE

You will now load Microsoft Excel using the Windows Start menu.

Setup: Ensure that you have turned on your computer and that the Windows desktop appears.

1 Position the mouse pointer over the Start button (🏁Start) appearing in the bottom left-hand corner of the Windows taskbar and then click the left mouse button once. The Start pop-up menu appears as shown here.

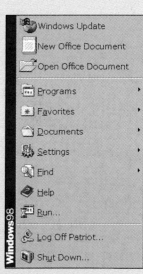

2 Position the mouse pointer over the Programs menu option. Notice that you do not need to click the left mouse button to display the list of programs in the fly-out or cascading menu.

3 Move the mouse pointer horizontally to the right until it highlights an option in the Programs menu. You can now move the mouse pointer vertically within the menu to select an option.

4 Position the mouse pointer over the Microsoft Excel menu option and then click the left mouse button once. After a few seconds, the Excel application window appears.

An Office Assistant character, like "Rocky" (shown at the right), may now appear. You will learn how to hide this character in lesson 1.1.2.

In Addition
Switching Among
Applications

Each application that you are currently working with is represented by a button on the taskbar. Switching among open applications on your desktop is as easy as clicking the appropriate taskbar button, like switching channels on a television set.

1.1.2 Touring Excel

FEATURE
The Excel **application window** acts as a container for the worksheet and chart windows. It also contains the primary interface components for working in Excel, including the *Windows icons, Menu bar, Toolbars, Name box, Formula bar,* and *Status bar.* The components of a worksheet **document window** include *Scroll bars, Sheet tabs, Tab Split box,* and *Tab Scrolling arrows.* Figure 1.3 identifies several of these components.

PRACTICE
In a guided tour, you will now explore the features of the Excel application and document windows.

Setup: Ensure that you've loaded Excel.

 Excel's application window is best kept maximized to fill the entire screen, as shown in Figure 1.3. As with most Windows applications, you use the Title bar icons—Minimize (▫), Maximize (▫), Restore (▫), and Close (☒)—to control the display of a window using the mouse. Familiarize yourself with the components labeled in Figure 1.3.

Figure 1.3

Excel's application window

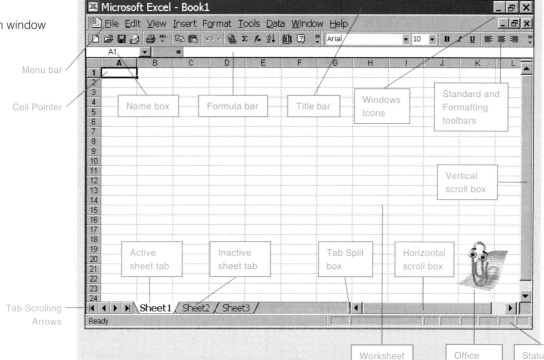

2 The Menu bar contains the Excel menu commands. To execute a command, you click once on the desired Menu bar option and then click again on the command. Commands that appear dimmed are not available for selection. Commands that are followed by an ellipsis (...) will display a dialog box. Pull-down menus that display a chevron (⟨⟩) at the bottom display further menu options when selected.

To practice working with the Excel Menu bar:
CHOOSE: Help
This instruction tells you to click the left mouse button once on the Help option appearing in the Menu bar. (*Note:* All menu commands that you execute in this guide begin with the instruction "CHOOSE.")

3 To display other pull-down menus, move the mouse to the left over other options in the Menu bar. As each option is highlighted, a pull-down menu appears with its associated commands.

4 To leave the Menu bar without making a command selection:
CLICK: in a blank area of the Title bar

5 Excel provides context-sensitive *right-click menus* for quick access to menu commands. Rather than searching for the appropriate command in the Menu bar, you can position the mouse pointer on any object, such as a cell, graphic, or toolbar button, and right-click the mouse to display a list of commonly selected commands.

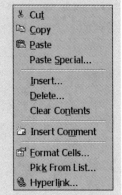

To display a cell's right-click menu:
RIGHT-CLICK: cell A1
The pop-up menu at the right should appear.

6 To remove the cell's right-click menu from the screen:
PRESS: ⌈ **ESC** ⌉

7 If an Office Assistant character currently appears on your screen, do the following to hide it from view:
RIGHT-CLICK: *the character*
CHOOSE: Hide from the right-click menu
(*Note:* The character's name may appear in the command, such as "Hide Rocky.")

1.1.3   Customizing Menus and Toolbars

FEATURE
Some people argue that software becomes more difficult to learn with the addition of each new command or feature. In response to this sentiment, Microsoft developed **adaptive menus** that display only the most commonly used commands. By default, Microsoft Office 2000 ships with the adaptive menus feature enabled. However, you may find this dynamic feature confusing and choose to turn off the adaptive menus. Likewise, the Standard and Formatting toolbars are positioned side-by-side in a single row by default. Again, you may find it easier to locate buttons when these toolbars are positioned on separate rows.

METHOD
To disable the adaptive menus feature:
1.   CHOOSE: Tools, Customize
2.   SELECT: *Menus show recently used commands first* check box, so that no "✔" appears

EXCEL

To display the Standard and Formatting toolbars on separate rows:
1. CHOOSE: Tools, Customize
2. SELECT: *Options* tab
3. SELECT: *Standard and Formatting toolbars share one row* check box, so that no "✔" appears

PRACTICE
In this lesson, you disable the adaptive menus feature and display the Standard and Formatting toolbars on separate rows.

Setup: Ensure that you've completed the previous lesson.

1 To begin, display the Tools menu:
CHOOSE: Tools
You should now see the Tools pull-down menu. When a desired command does not appear on a menu, you can extend the menu to view all of the available commands by waiting for a short period, by clicking on the chevron (⊻) at the bottom of the pull-down menu, or by double-clicking the option in the Menu bar.

2 Let's turn off the adaptive menus feature and customize the Standard and Formatting toolbars. Do the following:
CHOOSE: Customize from the Tools pull-down menu
SELECT: *Options* tab
The Customize dialog box should now appear (Figure 1.4.)

Figure 1.4
Customize dialog box

Customize toolbars

Customize Menu bar

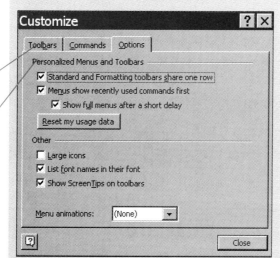

3 SELECT: *Menus show recently used commands first* check box, so that no "✔" appears

4 SELECT: *Standard and Formatting toolbars share one row* check box, so that no "✔" appears

5

To proceed:
CLICK: Close button

Figure 1.5 displays the Standard and Formatting toolbars as they should now appear on your screen. The Standard toolbar provides access to file management and editing commands, in addition to special features such as wizards. The Formatting toolbar lets you access cell formatting commands.

IMPORTANT: For the remainder of this learning guide, we assume that the adaptive menus feature has been disabled and that the Standard and Formatting toolbars are positioned on separate rows.

Figure 1.5

Standard toolbar

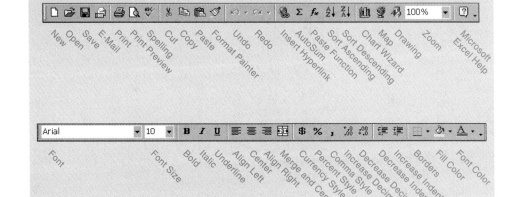

Formatting toolbar

In Addition Moving Toolbars	You can move toolbars around the Excel application window using the mouse. A *docked* toolbar appears attached to one of the window's borders. An *undocked* or *floating* toolbar appears in its own window, complete with a Title bar and Close button. To float a docked toolbar, drag the Move bar (|) at the left-hand side toward the center of the window. To redock the toolbar, drag its Title bar toward a border until it attaches itself automatically.

1.1 Self Check   How do you turn the adaptive menus feature on or off?

1.2 Creating Your First Worksheet

You create a worksheet by entering text labels, numbers, dates, and formulas into the individual cells. To begin entering data, first move the cell pointer to the desired cell in the worksheet. Then type the information that you want to appear in the cell. And finally, complete the entry by pressing (ENTER) or by moving the cell pointer to another cell. In this module, you learn how to navigate a worksheet, enter several types of data, and construct a simple formula expression.

1.2.1 Moving the Cell Pointer

FEATURE
You move the **cell pointer** around a worksheet using the mouse and keyboard. When you first open a new workbook, the cell pointer is positioned on cell A1 in the Sheet1 worksheet. Excel displays the current cell address in the **Name box,** appearing at the left-hand side of the Formula bar.

METHOD
Some common keystrokes for navigating a worksheet include:
- (↑), (↓), (←), and (→)
- (HOME), (END), (PgUp), and (PgDn)
- (CTRL) + (HOME) to move to cell A1
- (CTRL) + (END) to move to the last cell in the active worksheet area
- (F5) GoTo key for moving to a specific cell address

PRACTICE
You will now practice moving around an empty worksheet.

Setup: Ensure that Excel is loaded and a blank worksheet appears.

1 With the cell pointer in cell A1, move to cell D4 using the following keystrokes:
PRESS: (→) three times
PRESS: (↓) three times
Notice that the cell address, D4, is displayed in the Name box and that the column (D) and row (4) headings in the frame area appear boldface.

2 To move to cell E12 using the mouse:
CLICK: cell E12
(*Hint:* Position the cross mouse pointer over cell E12 and click the left mouse button once.)

3 To move to cell E124 using the keyboard:
PRESS: [PgDn] until row 124 is in view
PRESS: [↑] or [↓] to select cell E124
(*Hint*: The [PgUp] and [PgDn] keys are used to move up and down a worksheet by as many rows as fit in the current document window.)

4 To move to cell E24 using the mouse, position the mouse pointer on the vertical scroll box and then drag the scroll box upwards to row 24, as shown in Figure 1.6. Notice that a yellow Scroll Tip appears identifying the current row. When you see "Row: 24" in the Scroll Tip, release the mouse button. Then click cell E24 to select the cell.

Figure 1.6

Dragging the vertical
scroll bar

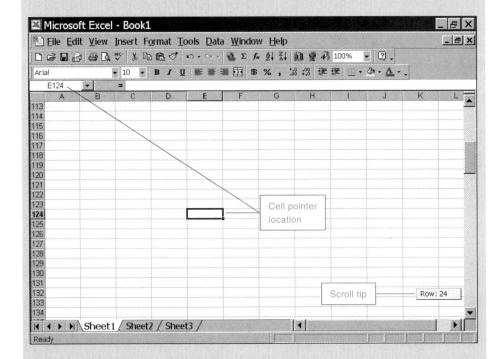

5 To move quickly to a specific cell address, such as cell AE24:
CLICK: once in the Name box
TYPE: ae24
PRESS: [ENTER]
The cell pointer scoots over to cell AE24. (*Hint*: Because cell addresses are not case sensitive, you need not use capital letters when typing a cell address.)

6 To move the cell pointer in any direction until the cell contents change from empty to filled, filled to empty, or until a border is encountered, press CTRL with an arrow key. For example:
PRESS: CTRL + ➡ to move to column IV
PRESS: CTRL + ⬇ to move to row 65536
The cell pointer now appears in the bottom right-hand corner of the worksheet.

7 To move back to cell A1:
PRESS: CTRL + HOME

1.2.2 Entering Text

FEATURE
Text labels are used to enhance the readability of a worksheet by providing headings, instructions, and descriptive information. Although a typical worksheet column is only eight or nine characters wide, a single cell can hold thousands of characters. With longer entries, the text simply spills over the column border into the next cell, if it is empty.

METHOD
TYPE: *a text string*
PRESS: ENTER

PRACTICE
In this example, you begin a simple worksheet by specifying text labels for the row and column headings.

Setup: Ensure that the cell pointer is positioned in cell A1 of the Sheet1 worksheet.

1 Let's begin the worksheet by entering a title. As you type the following entry, watch the Formula bar:
TYPE: Income Statement

2 To accept an entry, you press ENTER or click the Enter button (☑) in the Formula bar. To cancel an entry, you press ESC or click the Cancel (☒) button. To proceed:
PRESS: ENTER
Notice that the entry does not fit in a single column and must spill over into column B. This is acceptable as long as you don't place an entry into cell B1. Otherwise, you need to increase the width of column A.

After you press (ENTER), you may notice that the cell pointer moves to the next row. (*Note:* If your cell pointer remains in cell A1, choose Tools, Options from the Menu bar and click the *Edit* tab in the Options dialog box. Ensure that there is a check mark in the *Move selection after Enter* check box, as shown in Figure 1.7.)

Figure 1.7

Options dialog box: *Edit* tab

Ensure that this check box is selected and that the *Direction* drop-down list box displays Down.

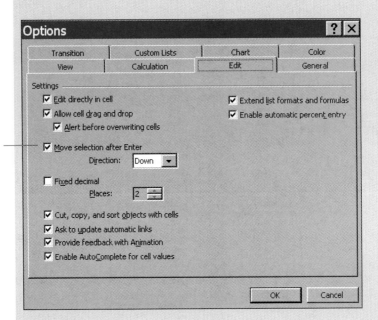

3 Move the cell pointer to cell B3.

4 Enter the following text label:
TYPE: **Revenue**
PRESS: ⬇
Notice that pressing ⬇ provides the same result as pressing (ENTER).

5 To complete entering the row labels:
TYPE: **Expenses**
PRESS: ⬇
TYPE: **Profit**
PRESS: (ENTER)
All of the text data has now been entered into the worksheet.

EXCEL

1.2.3 Entering Dates

FEATURE
You enter dates into a cell using one of the common date formats recognized by Excel, such as mm/dd/yy (12/25/99) or dd-mmm-yy (25-Dec-99). Excel treats a date (or time) as a formatted number or value. Consequently, you can use date values to perform arithmetic calculations, such as finding out how many days have elapsed between two calendar dates.

METHOD
TYPE: *a date*, using a recognized date format
PRESS: ENTER

PRACTICE
You will now add date values as column headings.

Setup: Ensure that you have completed the previous lesson.

1 Move to cell C2.

2 To enter a month and year combination as a date value, you use the format mmm-yy. For example:
TYPE: Sep-99
PRESS: ➡
(*Note:* Pressing ➡ moves the cell pointer one cell to the right.)

3 In cell D2, do the following:
TYPE: Oct-99
PRESS: ➡
TYPE: Nov-99
PRESS: ➡
TYPE: Dec-99
PRESS: ENTER
Your worksheet should now appear similar to Figure 1.8.

Figure 1.8

Entering date values into a worksheet

	A	B	C	D	E	F	G
1	Income Statement						
2			Sep-99	Oct-99	Nov-99	Dec-99	
3		Revenue					
4		Expenses					
5		Profit					
6							

4 Move the cell pointer to cell C2. Looking in the Formula bar, notice that the entry reads "9/1/1999" and not "Sep-99." As shown here, a cell's appearance on the worksheet can differ from its actual contents.

1.2.4 Entering Numbers

FEATURE

Numbers are entered into a worksheet for use in performing calculations, preparing reports, and creating charts. You can enter a raw or unformatted number, like 3.141593, or a formatted number, such as 37.5% or $24,732.33. It is important to note that phone numbers, Social Security numbers, and zip codes are not treated as numeric values, since they are never used in performing mathematical calculations. Numbers and dates are right-aligned when entered as opposed to text, which aligns with the left border of a cell.

METHOD

TYPE: *a number*, using recognized symbols
PRESS: ENTER

PRACTICE

You will now add some numbers to the worksheet.

Setup: Ensure that you have completed the previous lesson.

1 Move to cell C3.

2 To enter a value for September's revenue, do the following:
TYPE: 112,500
PRESS: ➡
Notice that you placed a comma (,) in the entry to separate the thousands from the hundreds. Excel recognizes symbols such as commas, dollar signs, and percentage symbols as numeric formatting.

3 In cell D3, do the following:
TYPE: 115,800
PRESS: ➡
TYPE: 98,750
PRESS: ➡
TYPE: 112,830
PRESS: ENTER

4 Move the cell pointer to cell C3. Notice that the Formula bar reads "112500" without a comma separating the thousands. Similar to date values, numeric values may be formatted to display differently on the worksheet than the actual value stored.

1.2.5 Entering Formulas

FEATURE

You use formulas to perform calculations, such as adding a column of numbers. A **formula** is an expression, containing numbers, cell references, and/or mathematical operators, that is entered into a cell in order to display a result. The basic mathematical operators ("+" for addition, "-" for subtraction, "/" for division, and "*" for multiplication) and rules of precedence from your high school algebra textbooks apply to an Excel formula. In other words, Excel calculates what appears in parentheses first, exponents second, multiplication and division operations (from left to right) third, and, lastly, addition and subtraction (again from left to right.)

METHOD

1. SELECT: the cell where you want the result to appear
2. TYPE: = (an equal sign)
3. TYPE: *the desired expression*, such as **A4+B4**
4. PRESS: (ENTER)

PRACTICE

You will now enter formulas into the worksheet that multiply the Revenue values by 60% to yield the related Expenses.

Setup: Ensure that you have completed the previous lesson.

1 Move to cell C4. Notice that the first step in entering a formula is to move to the cell where you want the result to display.

2 To inform Excel that you will be entering a formula, you type an equal sign. Do the following:
TYPE: =

3 In order to calculate September's expenses as 60% of the month's revenue, you multiply the cell containing the revenue value (cell C3) by 60%. Do the following:
TYPE: **c3*60%**
PRESS: ➡
The result, 67500, appears in the cell.

4 In cell D4, you will use a method called *pointing* to enter the required formula. With pointing, you use the mouse or keyboard to point to the cell reference that you want included in an expression. To illustrate:
TYPE: =
PRESS: ⬆
Notice that a dashed marquee appears around cell D3 and that the value "D3" appears in the Formula bar.

EXCEL

5 To finish entering the formula:
TYPE: ***60%**
PRESS: ➡
The result, 69480, appears in the cell.

6 For November's calculation, you will use the mouse to point to the desired cell reference. Do the following:
TYPE: **=**
CLICK: cell E3
Notice that cell E3 displays a dashed marquee to denote its selection.

7 To complete the row:
TYPE: ***60%**
PRESS: ➡
The result, 59250, appears.

8 Lastly, enter the formula for December by typing:
TYPE: **=f3*.6**
PRESS: **ENTER**
The result, 67698, appears in cell F4. Notice that you used the value .6 instead of 60% to yield this result. Your worksheet should now appear similar to Figure 1.9.

Figure 1.9

Entering formulas into a worksheet

	A	B	C	D	E	F	G
1	Income Statement						
2			Sep-99	Oct-99	Nov-99	Dec-99	
3		Revenue	112,500	115,800	98,750	112,830	
4		Expenses	67500	69480	59250	67698	
5		Profit					
6							

9 To illustrate the true power of Excel, you can change a cell's value and all the formulas in the worksheet that reference that cell are updated automatically. Do the following:
SELECT: cell F3
TYPE: **100,000**
PRESS: **ENTER**
Notice that the Expense calculation for Dec-99 (cell F4) is immediately updated to display 60000.

10 To conclude this module, you will close the worksheet without saving the changes. From the Menu bar:
CHOOSE: File, Close

11 In the dialog box that appears:
CLICK: No command button
There should be no workbooks open in the application window.

To display a new workbook and worksheet for use in the next module:
CLICK: New button (□) on the Standard toolbar
A new workbook, entitled Book2, appears in the document area.

1.2 Self Check Explain why a phone number is not considered a numeric value in an Excel worksheet.

EXCEL

1.3 Editing Your Work

What if you type a label, a number, or a formula into a cell and then decide it needs to be changed? Both novices and experts alike make data entry errors when creating a worksheet. Fortunately, Excel provides several features for editing information that has already been entered. In this module, you learn how to modify existing cell entries, erase the contents of a cell, and undo a command or typing error.

1.3.1 Editing a Cell's Contents

FEATURE
You can edit information either as you type or after you have entered data into a cell. Effective editing of a worksheet is an extremely valuable skill. In fact, few worksheets are created from scratch in favor of simply revising older worksheets. And, as a relatively new user of Excel, you will often find yourself engaged in modifying and maintaining worksheets created by other people.

METHOD
*   To edit data as you type, press (BACKSPACE) and then correct the typographical error or spelling mistake.
*   To replace a cell's contents entirely, select the cell and then type over the original data.
*   To edit a cell whose contents are too long or complicated to retype, double-click the cell to perform **in-cell editing.** In this mode, the flashing insertion point appears ready for editing inside the cell. Alternatively, you can press the (F2) EDIT key or click in the Formula bar to enter Edit mode, in which case you edit the cell's contents in the Formula bar. Regardless, once the insertion point appears, you perform your edits using the arrow keys, (DELETE), and (BACKSPACE).

PRACTICE

In this lesson, you create a simple inventory worksheet. Then, you practice modifying the data stored in the worksheet cells.

Setup: Ensure that a blank worksheet appears in the application window.

1   SELECT: cell A1
(*Note:* For the remainder of this guide, you may use either the keyboard or mouse to move the cell pointer.)

2   Let's enter a title for this worksheet:
TYPE: Staples Food Supplies
PRESS: ⬇
TYPE: Inventory List
PRESS: ENTER

3   SELECT: cell A4

4   Now let's add some column headings:
TYPE: Code
PRESS: ➡
TYPE: Product
PRESS: ➡
TYPE: Quantity
PRESS: ➡
TYPE: Price
PRESS: ENTER

5   On your own, complete the worksheet as displayed in Figure 1.10. If you make a typing error, use BACKSPACE to correct your mistake prior to pressing ENTER or an arrow key.

Figure 1.10

Creating an inventory worksheet

	A	B	C	D	E
1	Staples Food Supplies				
2	Inventory List				
3					
4	Code	Product	Quantity	Price	
5	AP01B	Apples	200	0.17	
6	DM21P	Milk	40	2.28	
7	DB29G	Butter	35	3.91	
8	FL78K	Flour	78	1.25	
9	RS04G	Sugar	290	7.23	
10					
11					

6 As the editor for this worksheet, you've noticed that the column heading in cell D4 should read "Cost" and not "Price." To replace this entry:
SELECT: cell D4
TYPE: **Cost**
PRESS: (ENTER)
Notice that the new entry overwrites the existing entry.

7 You activate in-cell editing by double-clicking a cell. To practice, let's change the quantity of butter from 35 to 350 packages:
DOUBLE-CLICK: cell C7

Notice that the Status bar now reads "Edit" in the bottom left-hand corner, instead of the word "Ready." A flashing insertion point should also appear inside the cell.

8 To add a "0" to the end of the cell's contents:
PRESS: (END) to move the insertion point to the far right
TYPE: **0**
PRESS: (ENTER)
Notice that the Status bar once again reads "Ready."

9 You can also activate Edit mode by pressing the (F2) EDIT key or by clicking the I-beam mouse pointer inside the Formula bar. In this step, you edit one of the product codes. Do the following:
SELECT: cell A6
Notice that the text "DM21P" appears in the Formula bar.

10 To modify the "DM" to read "DN," position the I-beam mouse pointer over the Formula bar entry, immediately to the left of the letter "M." Click the left mouse button and drag the mouse pointer to the right until the "M" is highlighted. Now that the desired letter is selected:
TYPE: **N**
PRESS: (ENTER)
The letter "N" replaces the selected letter in the Formula bar.

1.3.2 Erasing a Cell

FEATURE
You can quickly erase a single cell, a group of cells, or the entire worksheet with a few simple keystrokes. To erase a cell's contents, select the cell and then press (DELETE). If you would like to delete other characteristics of a cell, such as formatting attributes or attached comments, choose the Edit, Clear command from the Menu bar.

METHOD
After choosing the Edit, Clear command, select one of the following:
- *All*   Removes the cell contents, formatting, and comments
- *Formats*   Removes the cell formatting only
- *Contents*   Removes the cell contents only; same as pressing (DELETE)
- *Comments* Removes the cell comments only

PRACTICE
You will now practice erasing information that is stored in the inventory worksheet.

Setup: Ensure that you have completed the previous lesson.

1 SELECT: cell A2

2 To delete the subtitle:
PRESS: (DELETE)
Notice that you need not press (ENTER) or any other confirmation key. Pressing (DELETE) removes the contents of the cell immediately.

3 SELECT: cell A9

4 In order to delete a group of cells, you must first select the cells. In this step, you select the inventory line item for Sugar. Do the following:
PRESS: (SHIFT) and hold it down
CLICK: cell D9
RELEASE: (SHIFT)
The four cells should now appear highlighted, as shown in Figure 1.11.

Figure 1.11
Selecting a group of cells to erase

	A	B	C	D	E
1	Staples Food Supplies				
2					
3					
4	Code	Product	Quantity	Cost	
5	AP01B	Apples	200	0.17	
6	DN21P	Milk	40	2.28	
7	DB29G	Butter	350	3.91	
8	FL78K	Flour	78	1.25	
9	RS04G	Sugar	290	7.23	
10					

5 To erase all of the cell information:
CHOOSE: Edit, Clear from the Menu bar
CHOOSE: All from the cascading menu

6 PRESS: CTRL + HOME to move the cell pointer to cell A1

1.3.3 Using Undo and Redo

FEATURE

The **Undo command** allows you to cancel up to your last 16 actions. The command is most useful for immediately reversing a command or modification that was mistakenly performed. If an error occurred several steps before, you can continue "undoing" commands until you return the worksheet to its original state prior to the mistake. Although somewhat confusing, you can undo an Undo command. The **Redo command** allows you to reverse an Undo command that you performed accidentally.

METHOD

To reverse an action or command:
* CLICK: Undo button (⟲), or
* CHOOSE: Edit, Undo, or
* PRESS: CTRL + z

To reverse an Undo command:
* CLICK: Redo button (⟳)

PRACTICE

Let's practice reversing common editing procedures using the Undo command.

Setup: Ensure that you have completed the previous lesson.

1 SELECT: cell A5

2 In order to practice using the Undo command, let's delete the contents of the cell:
PRESS: DELETE

3 To undo the last command or action performed:
CLICK: Undo button (⟲) on the Standard toolbar
(*CAUTION:* The tip of the mouse pointer should be placed over the curved arrow and not on the attached down arrow.)

4 SELECT: cell C5

5 To modify the quantity of Apples:
TYPE: **175**
PRESS: ENTER

6 To undo the last entry using a keyboard shortcut:
PRESS: (CTRL) + z
The value 175 is replaced with 200 in cell C5. (*Hint:* This short-cut keystroke allows you to continue entering data without having to reach for the mouse or choose a menu command.)

7 Let's view the commands that Excel has been tracking for the Undo command. To begin, position the mouse pointer over the down arrow attached to the Undo button (⟲▾) on the Standard toolbar. Then click the down arrow once to display the drop-down list of "undoable" or reversible commands.

8 Move the mouse pointer slowly downward to select multiple commands. Your screen should appear similar to Figure 1.12.

Figure 1.12

Displaying reversible commands

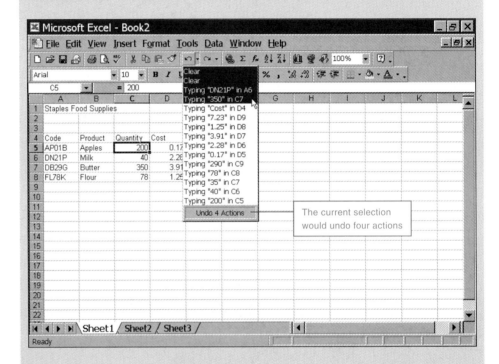

9 To remove the drop-down list without making a selection:
CLICK: down arrow attached to the Undo button (⟲▾)
(*Hint:* You can also click the Title bar, which provides a larger mouse target than the button's down arrow.)

10 To conclude this module, close the worksheet without saving the changes. Do the following:
CHOOSE: File, Close
CLICK: No command button

1.3 Self Check   Why is worksheet editing such a valuable skill?

1.4   Managing Files

Managing the workbook files that you create is an important skill. When you are creating a workbook, it exists only in the computer's RAM (random access memory), which is highly volatile. If the power to your computer goes off, your workbook is lost. For security, you need to save your workbook permanently to the local hard disk, a network drive, or a floppy diskette.

Saving your work to a named file on a disk is similar to placing it into a filing cabinet. For important workbooks (ones that you cannot risk losing), you should save your work at least every 15 minutes, or whenever you're interrupted, to protect against an unexpected power outage or other catastrophe. When naming your workbook files, you can use up to 255 characters, including spaces, but it's wise to keep the length under 20 characters. Furthermore, you cannot use the following characters in naming your workbooks:

$$ \backslash \quad / \quad : \quad ; \quad * \quad ? \quad " \quad < \quad > \quad | $$

In the following lessons, you will practice several file management procedures, including creating a new workbook, saving and closing workbooks, and opening existing workbooks.

Important: *In this guide, we refer to the files that have been created for you as the **student data files.** Depending on your computer or lab setup, these files may be located on a floppy diskette, in a folder on your hard disk, or on a network server. If necessary, ask your instructor or lab assistant where to find these data files. You will also need to identify a storage location for the files that you create, modify, and save. To download the Advantage Series' student data files from the Internet, visit McGraw-Hill's Information Technology Web site at:*

http://www.advantageseries.com

1.4.1 Beginning a New Workbook

FEATURE

There are three ways to start creating a new workbook. First, you can start with a blank workbook and then enter all of the data from scratch. Next, you can select a workbook **template** that provides pre-existing data and design elements. A template is a time-saver that promotes consistency in both design and function. And, lastly, you can employ a **wizard** to help lead you step-by-step through creating a particular type of workbook.

METHOD

- To display a new blank workbook:
  CLICK: New button (⬜)
- To begin a workbook using a template or wizard:
  CHOOSE: File, New

PRACTICE

In this example, you use one of Excel's prebuilt templates to create a new workbook for an invoicing application.

Setup: Ensure that no workbooks are displayed in the application window.

1 To view the templates that are available:
CHOOSE: File, New
The blank "Workbook" template icon appears on the *General* tab of the New dialog box. This workbook template is used by Excel when you click the New button (⬜) on the Standard toolbar.

2 The custom templates that are shipped with Excel and that have been installed onto your system appear on the next tab:
CLICK: *Spreadsheet Solutions* tab
Your screen should appear similar to Figure 1.13.

Figure 1.13

Displaying custom workbook templates

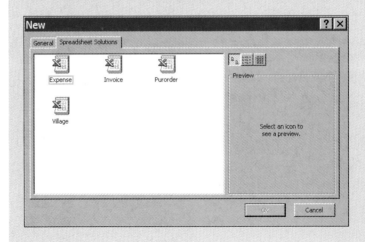

EXCEL

3 To create a new workbook based on the "Invoice" template:
DOUBLE-CLICK: Invoice template icon (📃)
(*Note:* If you or your lab administrator has not installed the
workbook templates, you must skip to step 7.)

4 A warning dialog box may appear stating that the template may
contain a **macro virus.** A virus is a hostile program that is
secretly stored and shipped inside of another program or document. As this template is provided by Microsoft and not from an
unknown source, you can safely enable the macros and continue:
CLICK: Enable Macros

5 If other warning dialog boxes appear, click the appropriate command buttons to remove them from the screen. You should now
see the Invoice template, as shown in Figure 1.14.

Figure 1.14

New workbook based on the
Invoice template

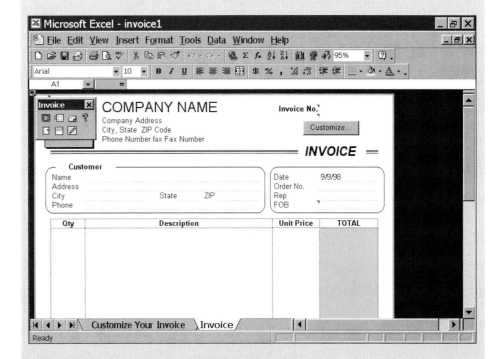

6 The workbook templates provided by Excel contain many
advanced features. Rather than introducing these features now,
let's close the workbook and continue our discussion of file management.
CHOOSE: File, Close
CLICK: No command button, if asked to save the changes

1.4.2 Saving and Closing

FEATURE
There are many options available for saving a workbook to a permanent storage location. The File, Save command and the Save button (▣) on the toolbar allow you to overwrite an existing disk file with the latest version of a workbook. The File, Save As command enables you to save a workbook to a new filename or storage location. Once you have finished working with a workbook, you close the file to free up valuable system resources (RAM).

METHOD
- To save a workbook:
  CLICK: Save button (▣), or
  CHOOSE: File, Save, or
  CHOOSE: File, Save As
- To close a workbook:
  CLICK: its Close button (☒), or
  CHOOSE: File, Close

PRACTICE
You will now practice saving and closing a workbook.

Setup: Identify a storage location for your personal workbook files. If you want to use a diskette, place it into the diskette drive now.

1 To create a new workbook from scratch:
CLICK: New button (▢)
TYPE: `My Library` into cell A1
PRESS: ENTER

2 To save the new workbook:
CLICK: Save button (▣)

(*Note:* If you have not yet saved a workbook, Excel displays the Save As dialog box regardless of the method you chose to save the file. The filenames and directories that appear in your Save As dialog box may differ from those shown in Figure 1.15.)

Figure 1.15

Save As dialog box

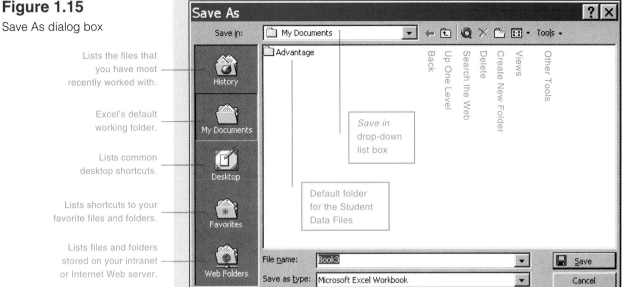

Lists the files that you have most recently worked with.

Excel's default working folder.

Lists common desktop shortcuts.

Lists shortcuts to your favorite files and folders.

Lists files and folders stored on your intranet or Internet Web server.

EXCEL

3. The **Places bar,** located along the left border of the dialog box, provides convenient access to commonly used storage locations. To illustrate, let's view the files in your "My Documents" folder:
CLICK: My Documents button (📁) in the Places bar

4. Let's browse the local hard disk:
CLICK: down arrow attached to the *Save in* drop-down list box
SELECT: Hard Disk C:
The list area displays the folders and files stored in the root directory of your local hard disk.

5. To drill down into one of the folders:
DOUBLE-CLICK: Program Files folder
This folder contains the program files for several applications.

6. To return to the previous display:
CLICK: Back button (⬅) in the dialog box

7. Now, using either the Places bar or the *Save In* drop-down list box:
SELECT: *a storage location for your personal files*
(*Note:* In this guide, we save files to the My Documents folder.)

8. Let's give the workbook file a unique name. Do the following:
DOUBLE-CLICK: the *workbook name* appearing in the *File name* text box to select it
TYPE: My Library

9   To complete the procedure:
CLICK: Save command button
Notice that the workbook's name now appears in the Title bar.

10   Let's close the workbook:
CHOOSE: File, Close

There are times when you'll want to save an existing workbook under a different filename. For example, you may want to keep different versions of the same workbook on your disk. Or, you may want to use one workbook as a template for future workbooks that are similar in style and format. Rather than retyping an entirely new workbook, you can retrieve an old workbook file, edit the information, and then save it under a different name using the File, Save As command.

In Addition
Creating a New Folder

Folders can help you organize your work. They also make it easier to find documents and back up your data. For example, you can use a folder to collect all of the workbooks related to a single fiscal period. You can also specify a folder to hold all of your personal documents, such as resumes and expense reports. While the Windows Explorer should be used for most folder management tasks, Excel allows you to create a new folder from the Save As dialog box. After you navigate to where you want the folder to appear, click the Create New Folder button ([image]). In the New Folder dialog box, type a name for the folder and press **ENTER**.

1.4.3 Opening an Existing Workbook

FEATURE
You use the Open dialog box to search for and retrieve existing workbooks that are stored on your local hard disk, a floppy diskette, a network server, or on the Web. If you want to load Excel and an existing workbook at the same time, you can use the Open Office Document command on the Start menu. Or, if you have recently used the workbook, you can try the Start, Documents command, which lists the 15 most recently used files.

METHOD
• CLICK: Open button ([image]), or
• CHOOSE: File, Open

PRACTICE
You will now retrieve a student data file named EXC140 that displays the market penetration for snowboard sales by Canadian province.

Setup: Ensure that you have completed the previous lesson. There should be no workbooks displayed in the application window. You will also need to know the storage location for the student data files.

1 To display the Open dialog box:
CLICK: Open button (📂)

2 Using the Places bar and the *Look in* drop-down list box, locate the folder containing the student data files. (*Note:* In this guide, we retrieve the student data files from a folder named "Advantage.")

3 To view additional information about each file:
CLICK: down arrow beside the Views button (📰▾)
CHOOSE: Details
Each workbook is presented on a single line with additional file information, such as its size, type, and date, as shown in Figure 1.16. (*Hint:* You can sort the filenames in this list area by clicking on one of the column heading buttons.)

Figure 1.16

Open dialog box

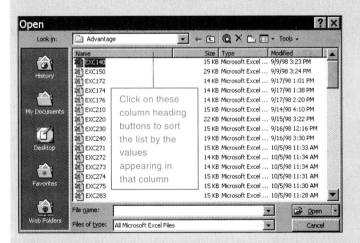

4 To return to a multicolumn list format:
CLICK: down arrow beside the Views button
CHOOSE: List

5 Let's open one of the workbooks in the list area:
DOUBLE-CLICK: EXC140
The dialog box disappears and the workbook is loaded into the application window. (*Note:* The "EXC140" filename reflects that this workbook is used in module 1.4 of the Excel learning guide.)

6 Now close the EXC140 workbook without saving the changes.

7 To exit Microsoft Excel:
CHOOSE: File, Exit

In Addition Opening and Saving Files of Different Formats	In the Open and Save As dialog boxes, you will notice a drop-down list box named *Files of type* and *Save as type* respectively. These list boxes allow you to select different file formats for opening and saving your files. For instance, you can save a workbook so that users with an earlier version of Excel are able to open and edit its contents. You can also open a file that was created using another spreadsheet software program, such as Lotus or Quattro Pro.

1.4 Self Check In the Open and Save As dialog boxes, how do the List and Details views differ? What two other views are accessible from the Views button?

1.5 Chapter Review

This chapter introduced you to using Microsoft Excel 2000, an electronic spreadsheet program. Spreadsheet software is used extensively in business and other industries for performing statistical analyses and summarizing numerical data for inclusion into reports. In the first module, you learned about worksheets and were led on a guided tour of the primary components in Excel. Next, you created a worksheet from scratch by entering text, numbers, dates, and formulas. The third module spent time explaining the importance of editing a worksheet effectively. In the last module, you learned how to create, save, and open workbook files.

1.5.1 Command Summary

Many of the commands and procedures appearing in this chapter are summarized in the following table.

Skill Set	To Perform This Task . . .	Do the Following . . .
Using Excel	Launch Microsoft Excel	CLICK: Start button ([Start]) CHOOSE: Programs, Microsoft Excel
	Exit Microsoft Excel	CLICK: its Close button ([x]), or CHOOSE: File, Exit
	Close a workbook	CLICK: its Close button ([x]), or CHOOSE: File, Close
	Customize menus and toolbars	CHOOSE: Tools, Customize
Managing Files	Create a new workbook	CLICK: New button ([D]), or CHOOSE: File, New
	Use a template to create a new workbook	CHOOSE: File, New CLICK: *Spreadsheet Solutions* tab DOUBLE-CLICK: *a template*
	Locate and open an existing workbook	CLICK: Open button ([⊞]), or CHOOSE: File, Open
	Open files of different formats	SELECT: a format from the *Files of type* drop-down list box in the Open dialog box
	Save a workbook	CLICK: Save button ([⊟]), or CHOOSE: File, Save
	Save a workbook using a different filename, location, or format	CHOOSE: File, Save As
	Create a new folder while displaying the Save As dialog box	CLICK: Create New Folder button ([⊡])

Continued

Skill Set	To Perform This Task . . .	Do the Following . . .
Working with Cells	Navigate to a specific cell	CLICK: in the Name box TYPE: *the desired cell address*
	Enter text labels, numbers, and dates	TYPE: *the desired entry*
	Enter a formula	TYPE: *=expression*
	Replace a cell's contents with new data	TYPE: *a new entry*
	Activate Edit mode to revise a cell's contents	DOUBLE-CLICK: the desired cell, or CLICK: in the Formula bar, or PRESS: `F2` EDIT key
	Delete cell contents	PRESS: `DELETE`
	Delete all information associated with a cell	CHOOSE: Edit, Clear, All
	Reverse or undo a command or series of commands	CLICK: Undo button (🔄), or CHOOSE: Edit, Undo, or PRESS: `CTRL` + z
	Reverse or undo an Undo command	CLICK: Redo button (🔄)

1.5.2 Key Terms

This section specifies page references for the key terms identified in this chapter. For a complete list of definitions, refer to the Glossary provided in the Appendix.

adaptive menus, *p. 10*   macro virus, *p. 29*

application window, *p. 8*   Name box, *p. 13*

cell, *p. 5*   Places bar, *p. 31*

cell address, *p. 5*   Redo command, *p. 25*

cell pointer, *p. 13*   template, *p. 28*

chart sheet, *p. 6*   Undo command, *p. 25*

document window, *p. 8*   wizard, *p. 28*

formula, *p. 19*   workbook, *p. 6*

in-cell editing, *p. 21*   worksheet, *p. 5*

1.6 Review Questions

1.6.1 Short Answer

1. Explain the difference between an application window and a document window.
2. What is the difference between a toolbar and the Menu bar?
3. What is the fastest method for moving to cell DF8192?
4. What is significant about how dates are entered into a worksheet?
5. How do you enter a formula into a cell? Provide an example.
6. With respect to entering a formula, explain the term *pointing*.
7. How would you reverse the last three commands executed?
8. How do you create a new workbook based on a template?
9. How would you save a copy of the currently displayed workbook onto a diskette?
10. How would you save a workbook in Excel using the Lotus spreadsheet file format?

1.6.2 True/False

1. ____ The cell reference "100AX" is an acceptable cell address.
2. ____ Pressing CTRL + HOME moves the cell pointer to cell A1.
3. ____ An Excel worksheet contains over 64,000 rows.
4. ____ Once a formula has been entered into a cell, you cannot edit the expression.
5. ____ A formula may contain both numbers and cell references, such as A1*B7-500.
6. ____ Pressing DELETE erases the contents of a cell.
7. ____ Pressing CTRL + x will undo the last command executed.
8. ____ You can create a new folder from within the Save As dialog box.
9. ____ You access Excel's workbook templates using the File, Open command.
10. ____ You can open files in Excel that have been created using different application software programs.

1.6.3 Multiple Choice

1. Which mouse shape is used to select cells in a worksheet?
   a. arrow
   b. cross
   c. hand
   d. hourglass

2. Excel displays the current cell address in the:
   a. Name box
   b. Status bar
   c. Title bar
   d. Standard toolbar

3. Using a mouse, you move around a worksheet quickly using the:
   a. Status bar
   b. Tab Scrolling arrows
   c. Tab Split bar
   d. Scroll bars

4. When you enter a text label, Excel justifies the entry automatically between the cell borders as:
   a. left-aligned
   b. centered
   c. right-aligned
   d. fully justified

5. When you enter a date, Excel justifies the entry automatically between the cell borders as:
   a. left-aligned
   b. centered
   c. right-aligned
   d. fully justified

6. Which keyboard shortcut lets you modify the contents of a cell?
   a. (CTRL)
   b. (SHIFT)
   c. (F2)
   d. (F5)

7. Which is the correct formula for adding cells B4 and F7?
   a. =B4*F7
   b. +B4+F7
   c. $B4:F7
   d. =B4+F7

8. To save the current workbook using a different filename:
   a. CHOOSE: File, Save
   b. CHOOSE: File, Save As
   c. CLICK: Save button (▣)
   d. CLICK: File, Rename

9. To open a new blank workbook:
   a. CLICK: New button (▢)
   b. CHOOSE: File, Open
   c. CHOOSE: File, Blank
   d. CHOOSE: File, Template

10. To reverse an Undo command:
    a. CHOOSE: Edit, Go Back
    b. CHOOSE: File, Reverse Undo
    c. CLICK: Reverse button (↶▾)
    d. CLICK: Redo button (↷▾)

1.7 Hands-On Projects

1.7.1 Grandview College: Semester Information

This exercise lets you practice fundamental worksheet skills, such as moving around a worksheet and entering text labels.

1. Load Microsoft Excel and ensure that a blank worksheet is displayed.
2. To enter a title label for the worksheet:
   SELECT: cell A1
   TYPE: **Grandview Community College**
   PRESS: (ENTER)
3. In cell A2:
   TYPE: **Enrollment Statistics**
   PRESS: ⬇ twice
   The cell pointer should now appear in cell A4.
4. Let's add some row heading labels:
   TYPE: **Courses**
   CLICK: cell A7
   Notice that when you click a new cell location, the contents are moved from the Formula bar into the cell as if you had pressed (ENTER).
5. TYPE: **Instructors**
   CLICK: cell A10
6. TYPE: **Students**
   PRESS: (ENTER)
7. On your own, enter the following text labels:
Move to cell	TYPE:
B5	**credit**
B6	**non-credit**
B8	**salaried**
B9	**contract**
B11	**full-time**
B12	**part-time**
8. To quickly move the cell pointer to the first column heading:
   CLICK: the Name box
   TYPE: **c4**
   PRESS: (ENTER)

9. In cells C4 and D4, enter the following column headings:
   TYPE: `Fall-99`
   PRESS: ➡
   TYPE: `Spring-00`
   PRESS: `ENTER`
10. To move the cell pointer to cell A1:
    PRESS: `CTRL` + `HOME`
11. Save the workbook as "Grandview Stats" to your personal storage location. (*Hint:* If you are unsure of where to store your personal files, select the "My Documents" folder.)
12. Close the workbook before proceeding.

1.7.2　Fast Forward Video: Store Summary

In this exercise, you will edit text labels in an existing worksheet, enter numbers and dates, and practice using the Undo command.

1. Open the data file named EXC172.
2. Save the workbook as "Video Stores" to your personal storage location.
3. To change the "Store" column heading to read "Location:"
   SELECT: cell B3
   TYPE: `Location`
   PRESS: `ENTER`
4. To correct a spelling mistake that occurs in the first location's name:
   DOUBLE-CLICK: cell B5
   PRESS: `END`
   PRESS: ⬅
   TYPE: `w`
   PRESS: `ENTER`
   The entry should now read "Downtown."
5. To expand upon the abbreviation used for the second location's name:
   SELECT: cell B6
   PRESS: `F2`
   PRESS: `BackSpace` to remove the last letter
   TYPE: `ream`
   The location name should now read "Coldstream."

6. To correct an error appearing in the second column heading:
    SELECT: cell D3

7. Position the I-beam mouse pointer to the right of the text in the formula bar and click the left mouse button once. The flashing insertion point should appear at the end of the word "Hour." Then do the following:
    TYPE: s
    PRESS: (ENTER)
    The entry now reads "Hours."

8. On your own, change the column heading "Tapes" to "Videos" and then correct the last heading so that it reads "Games."

9. Now let's put the current date on the worksheet:
    SELECT: cell D1
    TYPE: *the current date* using the format dd/mm/yy

10. Complete the following worksheet as shown in Figure 1.17.

Figure 1.17

Entering values into the Video Stores workbook

	A	B	C	D	E	F	G
1	Fast Forward Video			12/25/99			
2							
3		Location		Hours	Staff	Videos	Games
4							
5		Downtown		68	7	2,325	
6		Coldstream		68	5	1,790	
7		Westside		62	3	857	
8		Sahali Mall		74	9	2,114	
9							
10							

11. To delete the last column heading:
    SELECT: cell G3
    PRESS: (DELETE)

12. Now let's select the information for the Sahali Mall location:
    SELECT: cell D8
    PRESS: (SHIFT) and hold it down
    CLICK: cell F8

13. To erase all of the information in the selected cells:
    CHOOSE: Edit, Clear from the Menu bar
    CHOOSE: All from the cascading menu

14. To undo the deletion of the previous step:
    CLICK: Undo button (⟲▾) on the Standard toolbar

15. Save and then close the workbook.

1.7.3 Sun Valley Frozen Foods: Variance Analysis

You will now practice creating a worksheet from scratch that includes text, values, and formulas.

1. To display a new workbook and a blank worksheet:
    CLICK: New button ()
2. Enter the company name in cell A1:
    TYPE: **Sun Valley Frozen Foods**
    PRESS: ⬇
    TYPE: **Today is:**
    PRESS: ➡
3. Enter today's date in cell B2:
    TYPE: *the current date* using the format dd-mmm-yy
    (*Hint:* The date 9/24/99 would be entered as 24-Sep-99.)
4. Complete the worksheet as shown in Figure 1.18.

Figure 1.18

Entering data into a blank worksheet

	A	B	C	D	E	F
1	Sun Valley Frozen Foods					
2	Today is:	25-Dec-99				
3				Budget	Actual	Variance
4	Income					
5		Sales		43,000	41,380	
6		Service		17,500	19,620	
7						
8						
9	Expenses					
10		Materials		11,500	12,340	
11		Fixed Overhead		6,700	6,700	
12		Other Costs		12,500	12,975	
13						
14						

5. To calculate the Sales variance:
    SELECT: cell F5
    TYPE: **=e5-d5**
    PRESS: (ENTER)
    The value −1620 appears in the worksheet.
6. Using the same method, calculate the remaining variances for cells F6, F10, F11, and F12.

7. SELECT: cell C7
    TYPE: **Total**
    SELECT: cell C13
    TYPE: **Total**
    PRESS: (ENTER)
8. To sum the Income and Expenses columns:
    SELECT: cell D7
    TYPE: =
    SELECT: cell D5
    TYPE: +
    SELECT: cell D6
    PRESS: (ENTER)
9. Using either the typing or pointing method, enter addition formulas in the remaining cells of row 7 and row 13.
10. Save the workbook as "Sun Variance" and then close the workbook.

1.7.4 Lakeside Realty: Current Listing Report

This exercise lets you practice adding and modifying text, numbers, and formulas in an existing workbook.

1. Open the data file named EXC174.
2. Save the workbook as "Lakeside Listings" to your personal storage location.
3. In cell C7, you will now construct a formula to calculate the "Total Current Listings." Do the following:
    SELECT: cell C7
    TYPE: = **c3+c4-c5-c6**
    PRESS: (ENTER)
4. In cell A14, change the label from "Undeveloped" to read "Undeveloped Commercial."
5. In cell D14, you will enter the number of Undeveloped Commercial listings. As you do so, watch the formula in cell D16 recalculate after you press (ENTER). Do the following:
    TYPE: **19**
    PRESS: (ENTER)

6. The formula appearing in cell D16 for "Total Residential" incorrectly sums both the "Commercial" and "Undeveloped Commercial" listings. Therefore, you must edit the formula:
   SELECT: cell D16

7. Position the I-beam mouse pointer to the right of the formula in the Formula bar. Then, do the following:
   CLICK: the left mouse button and hold it down
   DRAG: the I-beam mouse pointer to the left to select "+D13+D14"

8. Once the selection is made, release the mouse button. Then:
   PRESS: DELETE

9. To complete the entry:
   PRESS: ENTER

10. In cell D18, enter a formula that adds up the Commercial (cell D13) and Undeveloped Commercial (cell D14) listings.

11. The Market Share column shows the proportional value of a particular row category as compared to either the Total Residential or Total Commercial results. To examine the formula used to calculate the Market Share for Single Family Houses, do the following:
    SELECT: cell F9
    Notice the expression displayed in the Formula bar.

12. Enter formulas in cells F10, F11, and F12 that calculate their respective market shares of the residential listings. (*Hint:* Divide each row value in column D by the Total Residential value in cell D16.)

13. Enter formulas in cells F13 and F14 that calculate their respective market shares of the commercial listings. (*Hint:* Divide each row value in column D by the Total Commercial value in cell D18.)

14. Save and then close the workbook.

1.7.5   On Your Own: Personal Monthly Budget

To practice working with text, values, and formulas, ensure that Excel is loaded and then display a blank workbook. You will now begin creating a personal budget. Enter a title that contains the words "My Monthly Budget." Under this title include your name and the current month. Now enter the following expense categories and a reasonable amount for each:

- Rent/Mortgage
- Food
- Clothing
- Car expenses
- Utilities
- Education
- Entertainment

In the same column as the labels, enter the words "Total Expenses." Then, beneath the column of numbers, enter a formula that sums the column. Now add a new column next to these budget figures that displays the percentage share for each budget category of the total expenses. For example, you would divide the value for Food by the Total Expenses value to calculate its share of the budget. Experiment with increasing and decreasing the budget expense figures to see their effect on the percentage share calculations. When completed, save the workbook as "My Budget" to your personal storage location and then close the workbook.

1.7.6   On Your Own: Personal Grade Book

To practice working with data and formulas, open the EXC176 workbook. Before continuing, save the workbook as "My Grades" to your personal storage location. Enter sample marks into column D of the worksheet.

Enter formulas that calculate the percentage grade for each test or assignment by dividing the "Mark" column by the "Out Of" column. Then, enter formulas that calculate the Term Percentages for display in cells F8 and F15. (*Hint:* Divide the total course marks achieved by the total marks possible.) Finally, enter a formula that calculates the average percentage of both courses for display in cell F17. Adjust some of the sample marks to ensure that the formulas are working correctly.

Save the workbook to your personal storage location. And, lastly, close the workbook and exit Microsoft Excel.

1.8　Case Problems: Rain Coast Air

Rain Coast Air, a small airline charter business on the West coast, is in the process of modernizing how it tracks and analyzes its business data. As an initial step, the new office assistant, Jennifer Duvall, is learning how to use Microsoft Excel. Her boss, Hank Frobisher, wants Jennifer to create a worksheet that will enable him to compare the monthly efficiency of each of his three planes. You see, Hank has an opportunity to purchase an additional float plane for well below market value. And, as a cost-conscious businessman, Hank wants to have a clear understanding of how his current equipment is performing before deciding to spend any money.

In the following case problems, assume the role of Jennifer and perform the same steps that she identifies. You may want to re-read the chapter opening before proceeding.

1. Jennifer decides to create a new worksheet that she can use as a template for each month's report. She begins by loading Microsoft Excel and displaying a blank workbook. Her first step will be to enter the title and the row and column headings. Then, the workbook needs to be saved to disk so that it can be later retrieved as a starting point for the monthly reports.

   Jennifer creates the worksheet shown in Figure 1.19 and then saves it as "Aircraft Stats" to her personal storage location.

Figure 1.19

The Aircraft Stats worksheet

	A	B	C	D	E	F	G	H
1	Monthly Aircraft Performance							
2								
3	Month:	Sep-99						
4								
5	Aircraft	Revenue	Expenses	Net Rev.	Flight Hrs	Rev/Hour	Exp %	
6								
7	XL-3079							
8	RB-2100							
9	DZ-514							
10								
11	Total							
12								
13								

2. Satisfied that this format will provide Hank with the information he needs, Jennifer begins to fill in the first month's figures. Then, she enters the formulas required to summarize each aircraft's performance. Most of the data she uses is taken directly from the monthly revenue and expense summaries prepared by the book-keeping service. The pilots' trip logs provide the rest of the data. After entering the data in Figure 1.20, Jennifer saves the workbook as "September Stats" to her personal storage location.

Figure 1.20

September's aircraft
performance report

	A	B	C	D	E	F	G	H
1	Monthly Aircraft Performance							
2								
3	Month:	Sep-99						
4								
5	Aircraft	Revenue	Expenses	Net Rev.	Flight Hrs	Rev/Hour	Exp %	
6								
7	XL-3079	15,326	4,259		87			
8	RB-2100	17,210	3,876		95			
9	DZ-514	9,845	2,633		53			
10								
11	Total							
12								
13								

3. Now, Jennifer tackles entering the formulas for the worksheet:

- She constructs formulas for display in row 11 that add the values appearing in the Revenue, Expenses, and Flight Hrs columns. The three formulas are entered into cells B11, C11, and E11.
- She enters formulas in cells D7, D8, D9, and D11 that calculate the Net Revenue by subtracting the Expenses for an aircraft from the Revenue it generated.
- She calculates and displays the Net Revenue per Hour in cells F7, F8, F9, and F11. The calculation she uses is simply the Net Revenue from column D divided by the Flight Hours in column E.
- Lastly, she calculates the Exp % column, which divides the Expenses by the Revenue and then multiplies the result by 100. She places the results in cells G7, G8, G9, and G11.

Unfortunately, Hank has already gone home. Jennifer decides to call it a day; she saves and closes the workbook. She is already looking forward to showing off her new creation to Hank in the morning.

4. The next morning, Jennifer opens the "September Stats" workbook and asks Hank to take a look at it. He is very pleased with the report and amazed at how quickly Excel can perform the calculations. Hank asks Jennifer what it would take to produce this report for another month. She explains that all she needs to do is enter the month's revenues, expenses, and flight hours into the appropriate cells; Excel then recalculates the worksheet automatically. Hank is outwardly impressed, realizing that he will finally have some decent information on which to base business decisions.

After mulling over the worksheet, Hank decides it would be prudent to purchase the fourth aircraft. With some minor modifications to the worksheet, he realizes that this information would come in handy during his meeting with the bank's loan officer. Hank calls Jennifer over to his desk and explains the revisions he wants her to make.

- The title of the report, explains Hank, should read "Rain Coast Air." And the aircraft should be identified by their names instead of their registration numbers. For example, the aircraft names are Eagle (XL-3079), Wanderer (RB-2100), and Sky Spirit (DZ-514).
- An upholstery repair bill for $262 was accidentally charged against the Wanderer, when it was actually for the Eagle. Therefore, the expense figures need to be adjusted accordingly. (*Hint:* To change the cell entry from a value to a formula, edit the cell contents by inserting an equal sign (=) at the front of the entry and "-262" at the end of the entry. You need an equal sign to convert the cell contents from a value to a formula.)

Jennifer makes the requested changes. She then saves the workbook as "Sept 99 Stats" and closes the workbook. As a last step, she exits Microsoft Excel.

MICROSOFT EXCEL 2000
Modifying a Worksheet

CHAPTER
TWO

Chapter Outline

2.1 Entering and Reviewing Data

2.2 Copying and Moving Data

2.3 Modifying Rows and Columns

2.4 Chapter Review

2.5 Review Questions

2.6 Hands-On Projects

2.7 Case Problems

Learning Objectives

After reading this chapter, you will be able to:

- Use several "Auto" features provided by Excel for entering and editing data and formulas

- Copy and move information with the Windows and Office Clipboards, and by using drag and drop

- Use the AutoFill feature and Fill commands to duplicate and extend data and formulas

- Insert and delete cells, rows, and columns

- Hide, unhide, and adjust rows and columns

Case Study

Granby Insurance Agency

The Granby Insurance Agency, located at the corner of 43rd and Main in Middleton's business district, is the city's largest private insurance company. Granby Insurance has always maintained a high profile in the community by sponsoring youth programs and providing assistance to the local charities. This sense of community was one of the main attractions for Scott Allenby, who recently joined the agency as their internal business manager.

Just last week, one of the agency partners purchased a new computer for Scott and made him personally responsible for generating the company's monthly profitability reports. With an increased workload, Scott knows that he must streamline operations and find a more efficient method for summarizing the data he receives. Fortunately, the computer came with Microsoft Excel installed and, after only a few days, Scott is now creating his own worksheets. Far from being comfortable with Excel's vast number of features, Scott has asked a knowledgeable friend to help construct a few simple workbooks for him to use.

In this chapter, you and Scott learn to modify and manipulate worksheet data. In addition to copying and moving information, you are introduced to inserting and deleting cells, rows, and columns. You also learn how to hide specific columns before generating reports.

2.1 Entering and Reviewing Data

Even novice users find it easy to build and use simple worksheets. In this module, you are introduced to some popular tools that can help speed your learning and improve your efficiency. Specifically, Excel provides three "Auto" features that may be used to enter repetitive data and perform calculations. Once you've practiced selecting ranges, you learn to use these three "Auto" features, called *AutoComplete, AutoCalculate,* and *AutoSum.*

2.1.1 Selecting Cells and Ranges

FEATURE

A **cell range** is a single cell or rectangular block of cells. Each cell range has a beginning cell address in the top left-hand corner and an ending cell address in the bottom right-hand corner. To use a cell range in a formula, you separate the two cell addresses using a colon. For example, the cell range B4:C6 references the six cells shown shaded below. Notice that the current or active cell, B4, is not shaded in this graphic.

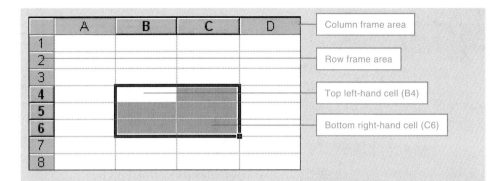

METHOD
To select a cell range using the mouse:
1. CLICK: the cell in the top left-hand corner
2. DRAG: the mouse pointer to the cell in the bottom right-hand corner

To select a cell range using the keyboard:
1. SELECT: cell in the top left-hand corner
2. PRESS: (SHIFT) and hold it down
3. PRESS: *an arrow key* to extend the range highlighting
4. RELEASE: (SHIFT)

PRACTICE
In this exercise, you open a workbook, save it to your personal storage location, and practice selecting single and multiple cell ranges.

Setup: Ensure that Excel is loaded.

1   Open the data file named EXC210.

2   In the next two steps, you will save the file as "My Gift List" to your personal storage location. Do the following:
CHOOSE: File, Save As
TYPE: **My Gift List** (but do not press (ENTER))

3   Using the *Save in* drop-down list box or the Places bar:
SELECT: *your storage location* (for example, the "My Documents" folder)
CLICK: Save command button
(*Note:* Most lessons in this guide begin by opening a student data file and then saving it immediately using a new filename.)

4   Let's practice selecting cell ranges. To begin:
SELECT: cell A3
(*Hint:* The word SELECT tells you to place the cell pointer at the identified cell address using either the keyboard or the mouse.)

EXCEL

5 To select the range from cell A3 to E3 using the keyboard:
PRESS: (SHIFT) and hold it down
PRESS: (→) four times
Although not explicitly stated in the above instruction, you release the (SHIFT) key once the range is selected.

6 The (CTRL) + (HOME) combination moves the cell pointer to cell A1. Pressing (HOME) by itself moves the cell pointer to column A within the same row. To move the cell pointer back to cell A3:
PRESS: (HOME)

7 To select the same cell range, but faster and more efficiently:
PRESS: (SHIFT) and hold it down
PRESS: (CTRL) + (→) together
Notice that the entire range is selected. You may remember from the last chapter that the (CTRL) +arrow combination moves the cell pointer until the cell contents change from empty to filled or filled to empty.

8 To select a cell range using the mouse:
CLICK: cell C6 and hold down the left mouse button
DRAG: the mouse pointer to E8 (and then release the button)
Notice that the column letters and row numbers in the frame area appear bold for the selected cell range, as shown in Figure 2.1.

Figure 2.1

Selecting a cell range

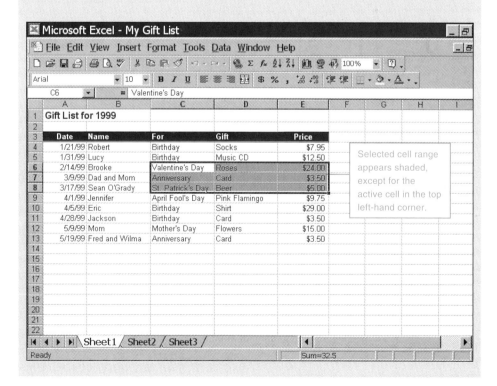

9 There is an easier method for selecting cell ranges for novice mouse users. To demonstrate, let's select the cell range from B10 to D13:
CLICK: cell B10
PRESS: [SHIFT] and hold it down
CLICK: cell D13
The range between the two cells should now appear highlighted. (*Note:* Remember to release the [SHIFT] key after the last selection is made.)

10 You can also select multiple cell ranges on a worksheet. To begin:
DRAG: from cell A6 to cell E6
PRESS: [CTRL] and hold it down
DRAG: from cell A9 to cell E9
You should see two separate cell ranges highlighted on the worksheet.

11 To select a third cell range:
PRESS: [CTRL] and hold it down
DRAG: from cell A12 to cell E12
(*Note:* Release the [CTRL] key after the last selection is made.)

12 To move the cell pointer to cell A1:
PRESS: [CTRL] + [HOME]

2.1.2 Entering Data Using AutoComplete

FEATURE
The **AutoComplete** feature second-guesses what you are typing into a worksheet cell and suggests how to complete the entry. After analyzing your first few keystrokes and scanning the same column for similar entries, AutoComplete tacks on the remaining letters when it thinks it has found a match. You can accept the Auto-Complete entry, or you can ignore its suggestion and continue typing. This feature can greatly reduce the number of repetitive entries you make in a worksheet.

METHOD
By default, the AutoComplete feature is turned on. If, however, you view its helpfulness as an intrusion, you can turn it off. To do so:
1. CHOOSE: Tools, Options
2. CLICK: *Edit* tab in the dialog box
3. SELECT: *Enable AutoComplete for cell values* check box to toggle AutoComplete on and off

PRACTICE
You will now practice using Excel's AutoComplete feature to enter data.

Setup: Ensure that the "My Gift List" workbook is displayed.

1 SELECT: cell A14

2 To add a new entry to the worksheet:
TYPE: 6/2/99
PRESS: ➡
TYPE: Anda
PRESS: ➡

3 You will now enter the word "Birthday" into cell C14. After typing the first letter, Excel notices that there is only one other entry in the column that begins with the letter "B" and, thus, makes the assumption that this is the word you want to enter. To demonstrate:
TYPE: B
Notice that Excel completes the word "Birthday" automatically.

4 To accept the completed word:
PRESS: ➡

5 For the remaining cells in the row:
TYPE: Shoes
PRESS: ➡
TYPE: $19.95
PRESS: (ENTER)
PRESS: (HOME)
Your cell pointer should now appear in cell A15.

6 Let's add another entry to the worksheet. Do the following:
TYPE: 6/5/99
PRESS: ➡
TYPE: Trevor and Ann
PRESS: ➡

7 You can use Excel's AutoComplete feature to display a sorted list of all the unique entries in a column. To illustrate:
RIGHT-CLICK: cell C15 to display its shortcut menu
CHOOSE: Pick From List
AutoComplete generates the list and then displays its results in a pop-up list box, as shown in Figure 2.2.

Figure 2.2

Entering data using the
AutoComplete pick list

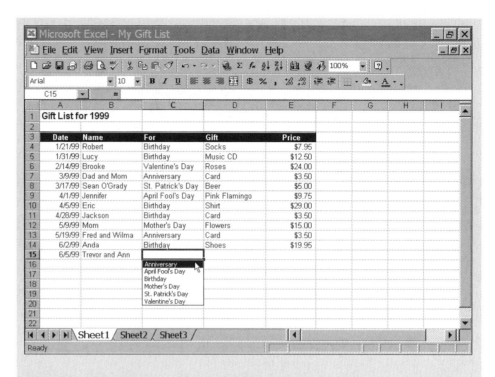

8 To make a selection:
CLICK: Anniversary in the pick list
(*Hint:* As a shortcut, press ALT + ↓ in a cell to display a column's pick list.)

9 To complete the row:
CLICK: cell D15
TYPE: **Picture Frame**
PRESS: →
TYPE: **$15.00**
PRESS: ENTER

10 Save the workbook and keep it open for use in the next lesson.
(*Hint:* The fastest methods for saving a workbook include clicking the Save button (🖫) or pressing CTRL + s.)

EXCEL

2.1.3   Using AutoCalculate and AutoSum

FEATURE

The **AutoCalculate** feature allows you to select a range of values and view their sum in the Status bar. This feature is useful for checking the result of a calculation without having to store its value in the worksheet. If, on the other hand, you need to store a result, click the **AutoSum** button (Σ) on the Standard toolbar. Excel reviews the surrounding cells, guesses at the range you want to sum, and then places a SUM function (described later in this book) into the current or active cell.

METHOD

- To use the AutoCalculate feature:
  SELECT: the range of values that you want to sum
- To use the AutoSum feature:
  SELECT: the cell where you want the result to appear
  CLICK: AutoSum button (Σ)

PRACTICE

Using the same worksheet, you will now practice viewing Auto-Calculate results and entering an addition formula using AutoSum.

Setup: Ensure that you have completed the previous lessons in this module and that the "My Gift List" workbook is displayed.

1 Let's say you want to know how much money to set aside for gifts in April. To find the answer, do the following:
SELECT: cell range from E9 to E11
Notice that only the April values are selected in the "Price" column.

2 Review the Status bar information. Notice that "Sum=$42.25" now appears near the right-hand side of the Status bar.

3 Let's perform another calculation:
SELECT: cell E4
PRESS: SHIFT and hold it down
PRESS: CTRL + ↓
All of the cells under the "Price" column heading should now appear selected. Assuming that you completed the previous lessons, the Status bar will now display "Sum=$148.65," as shown in Figure 2.3.

Figure 2.3

Adding values using
AutoCalculate

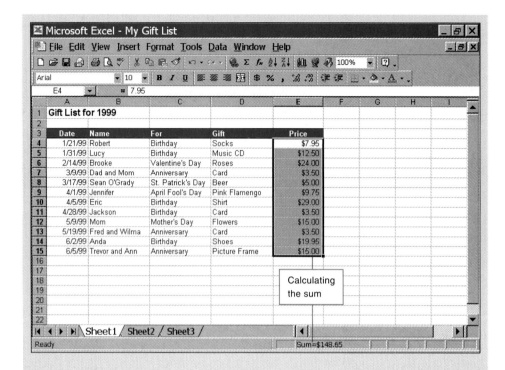

4 SELECT: cell D16

5 Let's enter a text label for the next calculation:
TYPE: **Total Cost**
PRESS: ➡

6 The quickest way to sum a row or column of values is using the AutoSum button (Σ) on the Standard toolbar. To demonstrate:
CLICK: AutoSum button (Σ) once
A built-in function called SUM is entered into the cell, along with the range that Excel assumes you want to sum. Notice that this cell range is also highlighted by a dashed marquee.

7 To accept the highlighted cells as the desired range:
CLICK: AutoSum button (Σ) again
The result, $148.65, now appears in cell E16. (*Note:* You could just as easily have pressed **ENTER** to accept the AutoSum entry.)

8 Perhaps you made a mistake in one of the column entries. To correct the mistake, do the following:
SELECT: cell E14
TYPE: **$119.95**
PRESS: **ENTER**
Notice that the AutoSum result in cell E16 now reads $248.65.

9 Save the workbook by clicking the Save button (🖫).

2.1.4 Inserting and Deleting Cells

FEATURE
You can insert a cell or cell range in the middle of existing data by moving the data that is there into the cells immediately below or to the right of the current selection. Likewise, you can delete a cell or cell range and close up the gap that is normally left when you clear the contents of a range.

METHOD
To insert a cell or cell range:
1. SELECT: the desired cell or cell range
2. CHOOSE: Insert, Cells
3. SELECT: *Shift cells right* or *Shift cells down* option button
4. CLICK: OK command button

To delete a cell or cell range:
1. SELECT: the desired cell or cell range
2. CHOOSE: Edit, Delete
3. SELECT: *Shift cells left* or *Shift cells up* option button
4. CLICK: OK command button

PRACTICE
You will now practice inserting and deleting cells.

Setup: Ensure that the "My Gift List" workbook is displayed.

1 Let's insert a new item into the worksheet list. To begin:
SELECT: cell range from A9 to E9

2 To insert a new range of cells:
CHOOSE: Insert, Cells
Your screen should now appear similar to Figure 2.4.

Figure 2.4

Inserting a range of cells

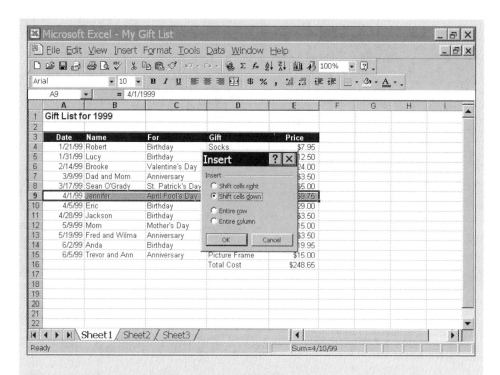

3 To complete the procedure, ensure that the *Shift cells down* option is selected and then do the following:
CLICK: OK command button
The existing data is pushed down to make space for the new cells.

4 Keep the cell range from A9 to E9 selected and enter a new item:
TYPE: **3/31/99**
PRESS: [ENTER]
Notice that the cell pointer moves to the next cell in the selected range.

5 To complete the row item with an Anniversary entry:
TYPE: **Tim and Starr**
PRESS: [ENTER]
TYPE: **An**
PRESS: [ENTER]
TYPE: **Mirror**
PRESS: [ENTER]
TYPE: **$37.00**
PRESS: [ENTER]
Notice that the cell pointer wraps around to the beginning of the selected range and that the "Total Cost" value in cell E17 is updated.

6 Now let's remove an item from the list:
SELECT: cell range from A12 to E12

7 To delete the selected cells:
CHOOSE: Edit, Delete
The Delete dialog box appears similar to the Insert dialog box shown in Figure 2.3.

8 To complete the procedure, ensure that the *Shift cells up* option is selected and then do the following:
CLICK: OK command button
The remaining cells slide up one row to close the gap and the "Total Cost" value in cell E16 is updated to $282.15.

9 PRESS: CTRL + HOME to move to cell A1

10 Save and then close the workbook.

2.1 Self Check Which of the "Auto" features enables you to sum a range of values and display the result in the Status bar?

2.2 Copying and Moving Data

Excel provides tools for copying, moving, and pasting data. Like the "Auto" features, these tools can help you reduce the number of repetitive entries you are required to make. For example, once you enter a formula to sum one column of values, you can duplicate that formula to sum the adjacent columns. There are three methods for copying and moving data. First, you can cut or copy a single piece of data from any application and store it on the **Windows Clipboard.** Then, you can paste the data into any other worksheet, workbook, or application. Second, you can use the new **Office Clipboard** to collect up to 12 items and then paste the stored data singularly or as a group into any other Office 2000 application. Lastly, you can use **drag and drop** to copy and move cell information short distances using the mouse. In this module, you practice duplicating cell contents and extending data and formulas in a worksheet range.

2.2.1 Using the Clipboards

FEATURE

You use the Windows and Office Clipboards to copy and move information within Excel and among other applications. The Windows Clipboard can store a single item of data from any application, while the Office Clipboard can store up to 12 items. (*Note:* The last item that you cut or copy to the Office Clipboard will appear as the one item stored on the Windows Clipboard.) When working in an Office 2000 application, such as Excel, you display the Office Clipboard toolbar by choosing the View, Toolbars, Clipboard command.

METHOD

Task Description	Menu Command	Toolbar Button	Keyboard Shortcut
Move data from the worksheet to the Clipboard	Edit, Cut	✂	CTRL + X
Place a copy of the selected data on the Clipboard	Edit, Copy	📋	CTRL + C
Insert data stored on the Clipboard into the worksheet	Edit, Paste	📋	CTRL + V

PRACTICE

Using the Clipboards, you will now practice copying data in a worksheet. The steps for moving data are identical to copying, except you use the Cut command instead of Copy.

Setup: Ensure that no workbooks are displayed in the application window.

1 Open the data file named EXC220.

2 Save the file as "Sales Forecast" to your personal storage location.

3 Let's sum the product values for entry into the Total row:
SELECT: cell range from B6 to D6
CLICK: AutoSum button (Σ)
The results appear immediately in the selected range.

EXCEL

4 You will now use the Copy command to duplicate data in the worksheet. To demonstrate:
SELECT: cell range from A2 to D6
Notice that all the data is selected, except for the title in cell A1.

5 To copy the range selection to both Clipboards:
CLICK: Copy button ( ) on the Standard toolbar
(*Note:* The range that you want to copy appears surrounded by a dashed marquee.)

6 You must now select the top left-hand corner of the location where you want to place the copied data. Do the following:
SELECT: cell A9

7 To complete the copy operation:
CLICK: Paste button ( )
The Paste button ( ) places the contents of the Windows Clipboard into the selected cell. The data, however, remains on both Clipboards.

8 Let's continue pasting the copied data into your worksheet:
SELECT: cell A16
CLICK: Paste button ( )
A second copy appears beneath the original data.

9 To demonstrate using the Office Clipboard toolbar:
SELECT: cell A1
CHOOSE: View, Toolbars, Clipboard
Your screen should now appear similar to Figure 2.5. (*Hint:* Unlike the Windows Clipboard, remember that the Office Clipboard can store up to 12 items and then paste them all at the same time.)

Figure 2.5

Displaying the Office
Clipboard toolbar

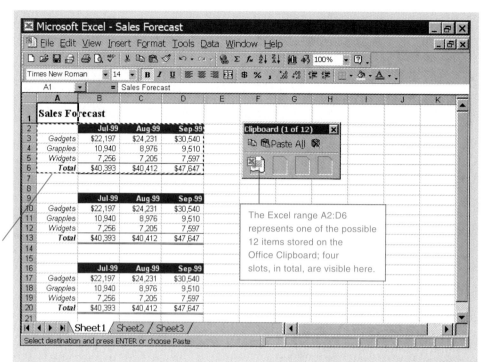

A dashed marquee
appears around the
range that has been
copied to the
Clipboard.

The Excel range A2:D6
represents one of the possible
12 items stored on the
Office Clipboard; four
slots, in total, are visible here.

10 To clear the contents of the Office Clipboard:
CLICK: Clear Clipboard button (🗷) on the Clipboard toolbar
Notice that the dashed marquee around the range also
disappears.

11 To add data items to the Office Clipboard:
SELECT: cell A3
CLICK: Copy button (🖼) on the Clipboard or Standard toolbars
SELECT: cell B3
CLICK: Copy button (🖼)
SELECT: cell C3
CLICK: Copy button (🖼)
SELECT: cell D3
CLICK: Copy button (🖼)
Depending on your screen resolution, your Office Clipboard may
expand to display an additional row of placeholders.

12 Position the mouse pointer over one of the data icons (🖼) in
the toolbar. A ToolTip will appear displaying the value stored in
the slot. Drag the mouse pointer over the other icons to see their
values. The data elements are stored in the order that they were
collected. You can paste a single item by selecting a target cell
and then clicking an icon in the toolbar. You can also paste all
of the items into a column format, as demonstrated in the next
step.

13 To paste all of the collected data elements into the worksheet:
SELECT: cell F9
CLICK: Paste All button (📋 Paste All)
(*Note:* You may need to move the Office Clipboard
window by dragging its Title bar before you can
select cell F9.) The contents of the Office Clipboard
are pasted into a single column in the worksheet;
each data element is placed into its own row, as
shown here.

Gadgets
$22,197
$24,231
$30,540

14 Let's prepare for another copy operation:
CLICK: Clear Clipboard button (🗑)

15 In this step, you want to collect, reorder, and then paste informa-
tion from Rows 3 through 5. The key to this step is to collect the
data in the order that you want to paste it later. For example:
SELECT: cell range A5 through D5
PRESS: CTRL +C
SELECT: cell range A3 through D3
PRESS: CTRL +C
SELECT: cell range A4 through D4
PRESS: CTRL +C
You should now see three occupied slots on the Clipboard
toolbar.

16 Let's paste the results over top of an existing data area in the
worksheet. Do the following:
SELECT: A10
CLICK: Paste All button (📋 Paste All)
Notice that you need only select the top left-hand corner of the
desired target range. Your screen should now appear similar to
Figure 2.6.

17 CLICK: Close button (☒) on the Office Clipboard toolbar

18 Save the workbook and keep it open for use in the next lesson.

Figure 2.6

Collecting and pasting
multiple items

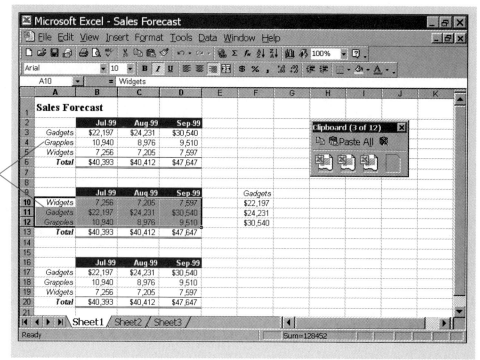

You can use the Office
Clipboard toolbar to
change the layout of
data in the worksheet.

2.2.2 Using Drag and Drop

FEATURE

You can use the mouse (and bypass the Clipboards altogether) to drag and drop data from one location in your worksheet to another. Although you cannot perform multiple pastes, the drag and drop method provides the easiest and fastest way to copy and move cell information short distances.

METHOD

1. SELECT: the cell range that you want to copy or move
2. Position the mouse pointer over any border of the cell range, until a white arrow pointer appears.
3. If you want to perform a copy operation, hold down the `CTRL` key.
4. DRAG: the cell range by the border to the target destination
5. Release the mouse button and, if necessary, the `CTRL` key.

PRACTICE

Using a mouse, you will now practice dragging and dropping a cell range in the worksheet.

Setup: Ensure that you have completed the previous lesson and that the "Sales Forecast" workbook is displayed.

1 Let's practice moving the data that was copied to column F in the previous lesson. Do the following:
SELECT: cell range from F9 to F12

2 Position the mouse pointer over a border of the selected cell range until a white diagonal arrow appears.

3 CLICK: left mouse button and hold it down
DRAG: mouse pointer upwards until the ToolTip displays "F2:F5"
Your screen should now appear similar to Figure 2.7.

4 Release the mouse button to complete the drag and drop operation.

Figure 2.7

Using drag and drop to move cell data

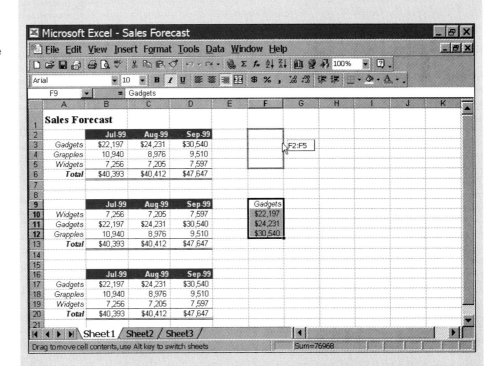

5 To copy a cell range using drag and drop:
SELECT: cell range from D9 to D13

6 Position the mouse pointer over a border of the cell range until a white diagonal arrow appears. Then, do the following:
PRESS: CTRL and hold it down
You should notice a plus sign is added to the mouse pointer.

7 CLICK: left mouse button and hold it down
DRAG: mouse pointer right to E9:E13

8 Release the mouse button and CTRL key to complete the copy operation. Notice that there are now two "Sep-99" columns.

9   SELECT: cell E9
TYPE: Oct-99
PRESS: [ENTER]
In one simple drag and drop operation, you successfully created
a new data column with the same formatting specifications as
the other monthly columns in the table.

10   Save and then close the workbook.

2.2.3   Creating a Series Using AutoFill

FEATURE
Excel's **AutoFill** feature allows you to enter a data series into a
worksheet. Whether a mathematical progression of values (1, 2,
3,...) or a row of date headings (Jan, Feb, Mar,...), a **series** is a
sequence of data that follows a pattern.

METHOD
1.   SELECT: the cell range containing the data you want to
     extend
2.   DRAG: the **fill handle,** which is a black square that appears
     in the lower right-hand corner of the cell range to extrapo-
     late the series
3.   Release the mouse button to complete the operation.

PRACTICE
In this exercise, you create a new workbook and then extend the
contents of cells using the fill handle and the AutoFill feature.

Setup: Ensure that no workbooks appear in the application window.

1   To display a new workbook:
CLICK: New button ([D])

2   Let's enter some source data from which you will create a series:
SELECT: cell A3
TYPE: Jan
PRESS: [↓]
TYPE: Period 1
PRESS: [↓]
TYPE: Quarter 1
PRESS: [ENTER]
Each of these entries will become the starting point for creating a
series that extends across their respective rows.

3 To extend the first entry in row 3:
SELECT: cell A3

4 Position the mouse pointer over the small black square (the fill handle) in the bottom right-hand corner of the cell pointer. The mouse pointer will change to a black cross when positioned correctly. (*Hint:* Figure 2.8 identifies the fill handle and mouse pointer.)

Figure 2.8

Using a cell's fill handle

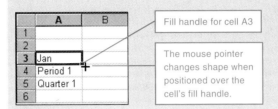

5 CLICK: left mouse button and hold it down
DRAG: the mouse pointer to column F, until the ToolTip displays "Jun"

6 Release the mouse button to complete the AutoFill operation.

7 Let's extend the next two rows:
SELECT: cell A4
DRAG: fill handle for cell A4 to column F
SELECT: cell A5
DRAG: fill handle for cell A5 to column F
(*Note:* Always release the mouse button after dragging to the desired location.) In the above example, notice that Excel recognizes the word Quarter; it resumes at Quarter 1 after entering Quarter 4.

8 You can also extend a date series using the fill handle:
SELECT: cell A7
TYPE: **Sep-99**
PRESS: ➡
TYPE: **Dec-99**
PRESS: (ENTER)

9 To extend the range using the same increment, you select both cells and then drag the range's fill handle. Do the following:
SELECT: cell range from A7 to B7
DRAG: fill handle for the range to column F
The quarterly values to Dec-00 appear.

10 You can also extract a nonlinear series from a range of values:
SELECT: cell A9
TYPE: **12**
PRESS: ➡
TYPE: **15**
PRESS: ➡
TYPE: **17**
PRESS: (ENTER)
Notice that there isn't a static incrementing value in this example.

11 To continue this range of values:
SELECT: cell range from A9 to C9
DRAG: fill handle for the range to column F
Excel calculates a "best guess" for the next few values. Your screen should now appear similar to Figure 2.9.

12 Save the workbook as "My Series" and then close the workbook.

Figure 2.9

Creating data series using the AutoFill feature

	A	B	C	D	E	F	G
1							
2							
3	Jan	Feb	Mar	Apr	May	Jun	
4	Period 1	Period 2	Period 3	Period 4	Period 5	Period 6	
5	Quarter 1	Quarter 2	Quarter 3	Quarter 4	Quarter 1	Quarter 2	
6							
7	Sep-99	Dec-99	Mar-00	Jun-00	Sep-00	Dec-00	
8							
9	12	15	17	19.66667	22.16667	24.66667	
10							
11							

Fill Handle

2.2.4 Extending a Cell's Contents

FEATURE
You use the Edit, Fill commands to extend a formula across a row or down a column. These commands allow you to copy a cell's contents to its adjacent cells in a single step. If you prefer using the mouse, you can also extend a cell's contents using its fill handle.

METHOD
1. SELECT: the desired cell range, ensuring that the data you want to copy is located in the top left-hand corner
2. CHOOSE: Edit, Fill, Right (or Left) to copy across a row
   CHOOSE: Edit, Fill, Down (or Up) to copy down (or up) a column

EXCEL

PRACTICE
In this exercise, you open a cash flow worksheet and then copy and extend the formulas that are stored therein.

Setup: Ensure that no workbooks appear in the application window.

1 Open the data file named EXC224.

2 Save the file as "Filling Cells" to your personal storage location.

3 To extend the date headings using the AutoFill feature:
SELECT: cell B1
DRAG: fill handle for cell B1 to column E
When you release the mouse button, the formatted date headings are entered into the columns.

4 In this worksheet, the beginning balance for a new month is the ending balance from the previous month. To enter this formula into column C:
SELECT: cell C2
CLICK: Bold button (B) to apply boldface to the cell
TYPE: =b11
PRESS: ENTER

5 To copy and extend this formula to the right:
SELECT: cell range from C2 to E2
Notice that the top left-hand cell in the selected range contains the formula (and formatting) that you want to copy.

6 CHOOSE: Edit, Fill, Right
For the moment, only zeroes will appear in the cells.

7 To extend the formulas for multiple ranges:
SELECT: cell range from B6 to E6
PRESS: CTRL and hold it down
SELECT: cell range from B10 to E10
SELECT: cell range from B11 to E11
When all the ranges are highlighted, release the CTRL key.

8 To fill each row with their respective formulas stored in column B:
CHOOSE: Edit, Fill, Right
Your worksheet should now appear similar to Figure 2.10.

Figure 2.10

Filling ranges with formulas
stored in the leftmost column

	A	B	C	D	E	F
1	Cash Flow	Sep-99	Oct-99	Nov-99	Dec-99	
2	Beg Balance	125,349	106,093	106,093	106,093	
3	*Add:*					
4	Cash Sales	45,000				
5	Receivables	15,234				
6	Total	60,234	0	0	0	
7	*Subtract:*					
8	Cash Exp	27,490				
9	Payables	52,000				
10	Total	79,490	0	0	0	
11	End Balance	106,093	106,093	106,093	106,093	
12						

9 On your own, enter sample values into the worksheet and witness how the formulas recalculate the totals.

10 Save and then close the workbook.

2.2 Self Check Which method would you use to copy several nonadjacent worksheet values for placement into a single column?

2.3 Modifying Rows and Columns

By adjusting the row heights and column widths in a worksheet, you can enhance its appearance for both viewing and printing—similarly to how a textbook employs white space or a document uses double-spacing to make the text easier to read. You can also reorganize or modify the structure of a worksheet by inserting and deleting rows and columns. This module shows you how to manipulate the appearance and structure of a worksheet.

2.3.1 Changing Column Widths

FEATURE

You can increase and decrease the width of your worksheet columns to allow for varying lengths of text labels, numbers, and dates. To speed the process, you can select and change more than one column width at a time. Excel can even calculate the best or **AutoFit** width for a column based on its existing entries. The maximum width for a column is 255 characters.

EXCEL

METHOD
- To change a column's width using the mouse:
  DRAG: its right borderline in the frame area
- To change a column's width using the menu:
  SELECT: a cell in the column that you want to format
  CHOOSE: Format, Column, Width
  TYPE: *the desired width*
- To change a column's width to its best fit:
  DOUBLE-CLICK: its right borderline in the frame area, or
  CHOOSE: Format, Column, AutoFit Selection

PRACTICE
In this lesson, you open a workbook used to summarize the income earned by organizers of a craft fair. Then you practice changing the worksheet's column widths to better view the data stored therein.

Setup: Ensure that no workbooks are open in the application window.

1 Open the data file named EXC230.

2 Save the file as "Craft Fair" to your personal storage location.

3 In columns D and E of the worksheet, you will notice that some cells contain a series of "#" symbols. These symbols inform you that the columns are not wide enough to display the contents. Let's adjust the width of column D using a command from the Menu bar:
SELECT: cell D1
Notice that you need not select the entire column to change its width; in fact, you can choose any cell within the column.

4 CHOOSE: Format, Column, Width
The Column Width dialog box appears, as shown here. Notice that 8.43 characters is the default column width.

5 Enter the desired width as measured in characters:
TYPE: **12**
PRESS: (ENTER) or CLICK: OK
All of the values stored in column D should now be visible.

6 Now let's adjust the width for column E. In the frame area, position the mouse pointer over the borderline between columns E and F. The mouse pointer changes shape when positioned correctly, as shown in Figure 2.11.

7 CLICK: the borderline and hold down the mouse button
DRAG: the mouse pointer to the right to increase the width to 12.00
Notice that the width (in characters and pixels) is displayed in a ToolTip. Your screen should now appear similar to Figure 2.11.

Figure 2.11

Changing a column's width

Microsoft Excel - Craft Fair

File Edit View Insert Format Tools Data Window Help

Arial   10   B I U

D1   =

Width: 12.00 (89 pixels)

Notice the change in mouse pointer shape when positioned properly.

	A	B	C	D	E	F	G	H
1	KETTLE VALLEY CRAFT FAIR							
2	Profit and Loss Statement							
3	Year Ending December 2000							
4								
5				This Year	Last Year	$ Chg	% Chg	
6	INCOME							
7	Booth Rentals			254,054.00	########	73,445.00	41%	
8	Advertising			44,700.00	########	2,700.00	6%	
9	Donations			1,525.00	1,745.00	(220.00)	-13%	
10	Other Income			0.00	0.00	0.00	0%	
11	TOTAL INCOME			300,279.00	########	75,925.00	34%	
12								
13	COST OF SALES							
14	Equipment Rentals			125,412.00	########	36,434.00	41%	
15	Brochure Printing			34,900.00	########	2,785.00	9%	
16	Other Direct Costs			0.00	0.00	0.00	0%	
17	TOTAL COST OF SALES			160,312.00	########	39,219.00	32%	
18								

8 Remember to release the mouse button to finalize the new column width setting.

9 The AutoFit feature enables you to find the best width for a column based on its existing entries. To adjust column A, let's select the entire column as the basis for the width calculation. Do the following:
SELECT: column A
(*Hint:* This instruction tells you to move the mouse pointer over the "A" in the column frame area and click once. When done properly, the entire column will appear highlighted.)

10 CHOOSE: Format, Column, AutoFit Selection
Notice that the width has been adjusted so that it can comfortably hold the longest entry in the column.

EXCEL

2.3.2 Changing Row Heights

FEATURE
You can change the height of any worksheet row to customize the borders and line spacing in a worksheet. What's more, a row's height is adjusted automatically when you increase or decrease the font size of information appearing in the row. A row's height is measured in points, where 72 points is equal to one inch. The larger the font size that you select for a given cell, the larger its row height.

METHOD
- To change a row's height using the mouse:
  DRAG: its bottom borderline in the frame area
- To change a row's height using the menu:
  SELECT: a cell in the row that you want to format
  CHOOSE: Format, Row, Height
  TYPE: *the desired height* in points
- To change a row's height to its best fit:
  DOUBLE-CLICK: its bottom borderline in the frame area, or
  CHOOSE: Format, Row, AutoFit

PRACTICE
You will now change some row heights in a worksheet to improve the spacing between data.

Setup: Ensure that you have completed the previous lesson and that the "Craft Fair" workbook is displayed.

1 SELECT: cell A1

2 In the next two steps, you will change the line spacing for the entire worksheet. As with most formatting commands, you must first select the object for which you want to apply formatting. In this case, you need to select the entire worksheet. To begin:
CLICK: Select All button (☐), as shown below

Click here to select
the entire worksheet.

	A
1	KETTLE VALLEY CRAFT FAIR
2	Profit and Loss Statement
3	Year Ending December 2000

3 With the entire worksheet highlighted:
CHOOSE: Format, Row, Height
The following dialog box appears.

4 In the *Row height* text box, enter the desired height as measured in points:
TYPE: **20**
PRESS: (ENTER) or CLICK: OK
Notice that the rows are enlarged, providing more white space.

5 To remove the selection highlighting:
CLICK: cell A1

6 Let's change the height of row 4 using the mouse. To do so, position the mouse pointer over the borderline between rows 4 and 5. Then:
CLICK: the borderline and hold down the mouse button
DRAG: the mouse pointer up to decrease the height to 9.00 points
Similar to changing the column width, the mouse pointer changes and a yellow ToolTip appears with the current measurement.

7 Release the mouse button to finalize the new setting.

8 Let's practice adjusting a row to its best height:
SELECT: row 5
(*Hint:* This instruction tells you to move the mouse pointer over the "5" in the row frame area and click once. When done properly, the entire row will appear highlighted.)

9 CHOOSE: Format, Row, AutoFit
The row height is adjusted automatically.

10 Save the workbook and keep it open for use in the next lesson.

2.3.3 Inserting and Deleting Rows and Columns

FEATURE
You insert and delete rows and columns to affect the structure of a worksheet. But in doing so, you must be careful not to change other areas in your worksheet unintentionally. Deleting column B, for example, removes all of the data in the entire column, not only the cells that are currently visible on your screen.

METHOD

- To insert or delete a row:
  RIGHT-CLICK: a *row number* in the frame area
  CHOOSE: Insert or Delete
- To insert or delete a column:
  RIGHT-CLICK: a *column letter* in the frame area
  CHOOSE: Insert or Delete

PRACTICE

In this lesson, you will practice inserting and deleting rows and columns.

Setup: Ensure that you have completed the previous lessons and that the "Craft Fair" workbook is displayed.

1 After adjusting the width for column A earlier in the module, you may have noticed that columns B and C do not contain any data. Before deleting rows or columns, however, it is always wise to check your assumptions. To do so:
CLICK: cell B1
PRESS: CTRL + ↓
The cell pointer scoots down to row 65536. If there were data in the column, the cell pointer would have stopped at the cell containing the data.

2 To check whether there is any data in column C:
PRESS: →
PRESS: CTRL + ↑
The cell pointer scoots back up to row 1, unencumbered by any cells containing data.

3 Now that you are sure that these columns are indeed empty, let's delete them from the worksheet. To begin, select both of the columns:
CLICK: column B in the frame area
DRAG: the mouse pointer right to also highlight column C
Release the mouse button after the two columns appear highlighted.

4 To delete these two columns:
RIGHT-CLICK: column C in the frame area
Notice that you need only right-click one of the selected column letters. Your screen should now appear similar to Figure 2.12.

Figure 2.12

Displaying the right-click
menu for selected columns

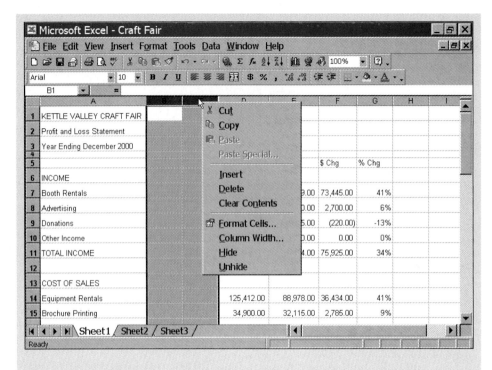

5 From the right-click menu:
CHOOSE: Delete
The column selection remains highlighted in case you want to
apply additional formatting commands.

6 To insert a row:
RIGHT-CLICK: row 8 in the frame area
CHOOSE: Insert
A new row is inserted at row 8; pushing down the existing rows.

7 To enter some new information:
SELECT: cell A8
TYPE: Food Pavilion
PRESS: ➡
TYPE: 55800
PRESS: ➡
TYPE: 43750
PRESS: ENTER

8 To copy the formulas for calculating the annual increase:
SELECT: cell range D7 to E8
CHOOSE: Edit, Fill, Down
The results, 12,050.00 and 28%, now appear in row 8.

EXCEL

2.3.4 Hiding and Unhiding Rows and Columns

FEATURE
Rather than deleting a row or column, you can modify a worksheet so that not all of the data is displayed. For example, you may want to hide rows and columns that contain sensitive data, such as salaries or commissions. You can even hide detailed information temporarily that you do not want included in a particular report.

METHOD
To hide a row or column:
1. RIGHT-CLICK: the desired row or column
2. CHOOSE: Hide

To unhide a row or column:
1. SELECT: the rows or columns on either side of the hidden row or column
2. RIGHT-CLICK: the selected rows or columns
3. CHOOSE: Unhide

PRACTICE
In this lesson, you practice hiding and unhiding worksheet information.

Setup: Ensure that you have completed the previous lessons and that the "Craft Fair" workbook is displayed.

1 Let's hide columns D and E from displaying. Do the following:
CLICK: column D in the frame area
DRAG: the mouse pointer right to also highlight column E

2 To hide the selected columns:
RIGHT-CLICK: column E in the frame area
CHOOSE: Hide
Notice that the column frame area now shows A, B, C, and then F.

3 To hide several rows in the worksheet:
SELECT: rows 7 through 11 in the frame area
RIGHT-CLICK: row 7 in the frame area
CHOOSE: Hide
PRESS: [CTRL] + [HOME] to move the cell pointer
The row frame area now displays a gap between row 6 and row 12. Your screen should now appear similar to Figure 2.13.

Figure 2.13

Hiding columns and rows

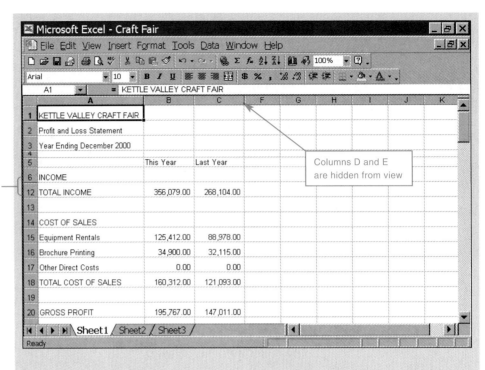

Rows 7 through 11 are hidden from view.

Columns D and E are hidden from view.

4. To unhide columns D and E, you must select the columns on either side. For example:
CLICK: column C in the frame area
DRAG: the mouse pointer right to also highlight column F

5. Let's use the Menu bar to unhide the columns:
CHOOSE: Format, Column, Unhide
The columns reappear on the worksheet.

6. To unhide the rows:
SELECT: rows 6 through 12
CHOOSE: Format, Row, Unhide
The rows reappear on the worksheet.

7. Save and then close the workbook.

8. Exit Microsoft Excel.

2.3 Self Check   Why must you be careful when deleting rows or columns?

2.4 Chapter Review

This chapter introduced you to some common procedures for modifying the contents and structure of a worksheet. In the first module, you entered data and formulas using Excel's special "Auto" features, including AutoComplete and AutoSum. Then you learned how to use the Windows and Office Clipboards and Excel's drag and drop features for moving, copying, and pasting data. You also practiced using the AutoFill feature by dragging a cell range's fill handle to extend a data series. As for modifying a worksheet's structure, you inserted and deleted cells, rows, and columns. And lastly, you practiced hiding, unhiding, and changing the height and width of rows and columns.

2.4.1 Command Summary

Many of the commands and procedures appearing in this chapter are summarized in the following table.

Skill Set	To Perform This Task . . .	Do the Following . . .
Using Functions	Entering the SUM function using the AutoSum button	SELECT: a cell to place the result CLICK: AutoSum button (Σ)
	Displaying the sum result of a calculation using AutoCalculate	SELECT: a cell range and view the result in the Status bar
Working with Cells	Insert a cell or cell range	SELECT: the desired cell range CHOOSE: Insert, Cells
	Delete a cell or cell range	SELECT: the desired cell range CHOOSE: Edit, Delete
	Insert data using AutoComplete	RIGHT-CLICK: the desired cell CHOOSE: Pick From List SELECT: the desired data
	Copy or move data using the toolbar	SELECT: the desired cell or range CLICK: Copy (🖹) or Cut (✂) SELECT: the target cell or range CLICK: Paste button (📋)
	Move data using drag and drop	SELECT: the desired cell or range DRAG: the selection by its border

Continued

Skill Set	To Perform This Task . . .	Do the Following . . .
	Copy data using drag and drop	SELECT: the desired cell or range PRESS: `CTRL` and hold it down DRAG: the selection by its border
	Display the Office Clipboard	CHOOSE: View, Toolbars, Clipboard
	Clear the Office Clipboard	CLICK: Clear Clipboard button (🗙)
	Create a series using the fill handle	SELECT: the desired range DRAG: the fill handle
	Copy a formula across a row or down a column	SELECT: the range to fill; with the formula in the top left-hand corner CHOOSE: Edit, Fill, Right (or Down)
Formatting Worksheets	Change a cell's column width	CHOOSE: Format, Column, Width TYPE: *width* in characters
	Change a cell's row height	CHOOSE: Format, Row, Height TYPE: *height* in points
Modifying Worksheets	Insert and delete columns	RIGHT-CLICK: a column's frame area CHOOSE: Insert or Delete
	Insert and delete rows	RIGHT-CLICK: a row's frame area CHOOSE: Insert or Delete
	Hide a row or column	RIGHT-CLICK: in the frame area CHOOSE: Hide
	Unhide a row or column	SELECT: rows or columns on either side of the hidden row or column RIGHT-CLICK: the frame selection CHOOSE: Unhide

3. The AutoSum feature enters this function into a cell to sum a range of values:
   a. ADD
   b. SUM
   c. TOTAL
   d. VALUE

4. If you want to delete cells from the worksheet, you select the desired range and then choose the following command:
   a. Edit, Clear, All
   b. Edit, Clear, Cells
   c. Edit, Cells, Delete
   d. Edit, Delete

5. To perform a drag and drop operation, you position the mouse pointer over the selected cell or cell range until it changes to this shape.
   a. ✚
   b. ✛
   c. ▷
   d. ✛

6. What menu command allows you to copy a formula in the active cell to a range of adjacent cells in a row?
   a. Edit, Fill, Down
   b. Edit, Fill, Right
   c. Edit, Copy, Right
   d. Edit, Extend, Fill

7. To select an entire column for editing, inserting, or deleting:
   a. PRESS: ALT + ↓ with the cell pointer in the column
   b. DOUBLE-CLICK: a cell within the column
   c. CLICK: the column letter in the frame area
   d. CHOOSE: Edit, Select Column

8. The height of a row is typically measured using these units.
   a. Characters
   b. Fonts
   c. Picas
   d. Points

9. To change a column's width using the mouse, you position the mouse pointer into the column frame area until it changes to this shape.
   a. ✚
   b. ✛
   c. ▷
   d. ✛

10. Row 5 is hidden on your worksheet. To unhide the row, you must make this selection before issuing the appropriate menu command.
    a. rows 4 and 6
    b. rows 1 through 4
    c. row 4
    d. row 6

2.6 Hands-On Projects

2.6.1 Grandview College: Course List

In this exercise, you practice using Excel's "Auto" features to enter information and calculate results.

1. Load Microsoft Excel.
2. Open the data file named EXC261.
3. Save the workbook as "Course List" to your personal storage location.
4. To complete this worksheet, you must enter some additional information for "Intermediate French." To begin:
    SELECT: cell B9
    TYPE: L
    PRESS: (ENTER)
    Notice that the word "Languages" is inserted automatically.
5. To enter some data for the "Writer's Workshop," do the following:
    RIGHT-CLICK: cell B10
    CHOOSE: Pick From List
    CLICK: English in the pick list
6. To use AutoComplete with the keyboard:
    SELECT: cell C10
    PRESS: (ALT) + (↓)
    PRESS: (↓) four more times to highlight "Molina"
    PRESS: (ENTER)
7. Now let's use the AutoCalculate feature to sum the total number of hours without placing an entry into the worksheet. Do the following:
    SELECT: cell range from D5 to D10
    Notice that the Status bar now displays "Sum = 169."

8. You will now enter a total formula for the Hours column:
   SELECT: cell D12
   CLICK: AutoSum button (Σ)
   CLICK: AutoSum button (Σ) a second time to accept the cell range
   The answer, 169, now appears in the cell.
9. On your own, place a total formula in cell E12 for the Credits column.
10. Save and then close the workbook.

2.6.2 Fast Forward Video: Top Five Rentals

You will now practice copying and moving data using Excel's AutoFill feature, drag and drop, and the Windows and Office Clipboards.

1. Open the data file named EXC262.
2. Save the workbook as "Top Five" to your personal storage location.
3. Let's use the AutoFill feature to extend the heading to column C:
   SELECT: cell B1
   DRAG: fill handle for cell B1 to column C
   Notice that the text entry becomes "Week-2" and that the formatting is also copied.
4. On your own, extend the column heading for Week-2 in row 8.
5. You will now extend the row labels for "Videos" in column A. Do the following:
   SELECT: cell range from A2 to A3
   DRAG: fill handle for the selected cell range to row 6
6. On your own, extend the row labels for "Games" in column A.
7. Using the Windows Clipboard, copy the first two videos from Week-1 (Rocky: the Next Generation and Lethal Instinct) to the same positions in Week-2:
   SELECT: cell range from B2 to B3
   CLICK: Copy button ($\boxed{\text{copy}}$) on the Standard toolbar
   SELECT: cell C2
   CLICK: Paste button ($\boxed{\text{paste}}$)
   PRESS: ESC to remove the dashed marquee
8. Using drag and drop, copy the number 3 video of Week-1 (Rent: the Movie) to the number 5 position of Week-2:
   SELECT: cell B3

9. Position the mouse pointer over the border of the selected cell so that a white diagonal arrow appears. Then, do the following:
PRESS: (CTRL) and hold it down
DRAG: mouse pointer to cell C6

10. Release the mouse button and then the (CTRL) key to complete the copy operation.

11. Using drag and drop, copy the cell range B5:B6 (X-Files 2 and Wild and Crazy Guys) to cells C4:C5.

12. You will use the Office Clipboard to modify the Games order from Week-1 to Week-2. First, display the Office Clipboard toolbar and clear its existing contents:
CHOOSE: View, Toolbars, Clipboard
CLICK: Clear Clipboard button (🗙) on the Clipboard toolbar

13. Now, add the Games to the Office Clipboard:
SELECT: cell B12
CLICK: Copy button (🗐) on the Clipboard or Standard toolbars
SELECT: cell B9
CLICK: Copy button (🗐)
SELECT: cell B10
CLICK: Copy button (🗐)
SELECT: cell B13
CLICK: Copy button (🗐)
SELECT: cell B11
CLICK: Copy button (🗐)

14. Now, paste all of the data elements into the Week-2 column:
SELECT: cell C9
CLICK: Paste All button (🗐 Paste All)
Your screen should now appear similar to Figure 2.14.

15. Lastly, remove the range selection highlighting and close the Office Clipboard toolbar:
PRESS: (CTRL) + (HOME)
CLICK: Close button on the Office Clipboard toolbar

16. Save and then close the "Top Five" workbook.

Figure 2.14

Pasting data from
the Office Clipboard

2.6.3 Sun Valley Frozen Foods: Sales Force

In this exercise, you practice modifying an existing worksheet that is
used to track sales representatives for Sun Valley Frozen Foods.

1. Open the data file named EXC263.
2. Save the workbook as "Sales Force" to your personal storage
   location.
3. You may have noticed that the title in cell A1 is difficult to
   read. Adjust the height for row 1 to its "best fit" or "AutoFit"
   height.
4. The sales representatives' names are truncated by the "Location" entries in column B. Therefore, adjust the width of column A to ensure that all the names are visible.
5. Change the column width for columns B through D to 8
   characters.
6. Change the column width for columns E through G to 10
   characters.
7. Change the height of rows 2 through 15 to 15.00.
8. In cell F4, enter a commission rate of 5%.
9. In cell G4, multiply the commission rate (F) by the
   Revenue (E).
10. Copy the entries in cells F4 and G4 down the column to
    row 15.
11. Remove the Route information by deleting column C.
12. Remove the information for Bruce Towne by deleting the cell
    range A8 to F8 and then closing up the gap.

13. Hide the two end columns used in calculating and displaying a sales rep's commission.
14. Without placing a formula on the worksheet, calculate the total Revenue collected by these sales reps. What is this value?
15. Save and then close the workbook.

2.6.4 Lakeside Realty: Sales Projections

In this exercise, you practice copying data and modifying a worksheet.

1. Open the data file named EXC264.
2. Save the workbook as "Sales Volume" to your personal storage location.
3. Increase the width of column A to 12 characters.
4. Use the AutoSum button to sum the values for columns B through D and display the results in row 9.
5. To extend the table to project values for the years 2000, 2001, and 2002, select the cell range from B4 to D9.
6. Drag the fill handle of the selected range to column G. When you release the mouse button, the range is filled with projected results. These results are based on the trends calculated from the selected columns of data. Notice that you did not enter any formulas into the worksheet, other than using AutoSum to provide a totals row.
7. Use the Office Clipboard to collect and sort data from the worksheet and then paste the results into the area below the table. Specifically, replicate the result shown in Figure 2.15.

Figure 2.15

Using the Office Clipboard to organize data

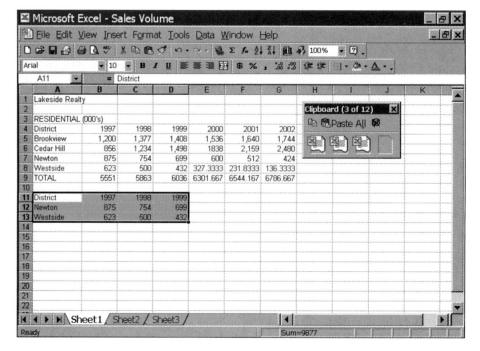

8. Clear the Clipboard contents and then close the Clipboard toolbar.
9. Hide rows 4 through 8.
10. Save and then close the workbook.

2.6.5 On Your Own: Blue Zone Personnel

A friend of yours has just accepted a position at Blue Zone Personnel. In addition to her general administrative duties, she must help the accountant prepare monthly income statements. Since she seemed quite nervous about the new position, you offered to help her develop an Excel worksheet. You open the EXC265 workbook that she has been using and save it as "Blue Zone" to her personal storage location.

After adjusting the column widths, you review the structure of the worksheet. To begin, you insert a row above EXPENSES and label it Total Revenue. Then, you use the AutoSum feature to sum the revenues for September and October. Continuing in this manner, you adjust and insert rows, data, and formulas so that the worksheet appears similar to Figure 2.16. Then, you save and close the workbook.

Figure 2.16

Modifying a worksheet's structure and appearance

	A	B	C	D
1	Blue Zone Personnel			
2				
3	REVENUE	Sep-99	Oct-99	
4	Programming	12,400	13,100	
5	Service Calls	450	540	
6	Technical Support	225	330	
7	Total Revenue	13,075	13,970	
8	EXPENSES			
9	Advertising	200	250	
10	Bank Charges	25	25	
11	Depreciation	2,400	2,400	
12	Payroll Costs	10,000	10,000	
13	Telephone	275	275	
14	Total Expenses	12900	12950	
15	PROFIT	175	1,020	
16				

AutoSum formula (row 7)
New row inserted (row 9)
AutoSum formula (row 14)
Subtraction formula (row 15)

2.6.6 On Your Own: Running Diary

It's May and you're finally getting around to that New Year's resolution of getting into shape. To motivate yourself, you decide to create a running diary using Microsoft Excel. Open the data file named EXC266 and then save it as "My Running Diary" to your personal storage location.

Given your current statistics, you'd like to project how long it will take you to reach 10 miles. To do so, you select the cell range from B4 through B12. Then drag the fill handle for the range downward until the ToolTip displays a value over 10. You then press CTRL + HOME to return to the top of the worksheet. To make it easier to count the number of runs, you insert a new column A and then number each run in the column using the fill handle. *How many runs will it take you to reach 10 miles?* You then use Excel's AutoCalculate feature to determine how many total miles you have run as of May 23rd. *How many miles have you run thus far?* Impressed with your computer knowledge, your running partner asks you to track her running statistics also. Rather than create a new worksheet, you copy and paste the column headings beside your own, so that they begin in column H. Lastly, you save and close the workbook and then exit Excel.

2.7 Case Problems: Granby Insurance Agency

Scott Allenby, the business manager for the Granby Insurance Agency, is responsible for generating monthly profitability reports. One of the key business areas for Granby involves a long-standing agreement with a local car dealer to manage their financing, insurance, and after-market sales. Upon reviewing some of the past data from the dealership, Scott identifies an opportunity to use Microsoft Excel for generating their reports.

In the following case problems, assume the role of Scott and perform the same steps that he identifies. You may want to re-read the chapter opening before proceeding.

1. Scott decides to focus his attention on one report that is generated for the car dealership at the end of each month. He calls a good friend, whom he knows has several months experience using Excel, and describes what he needs over the phone. He then sends him a fax of the actual report to help clarify the discussion. The next day, Scott receives a diskette from his friend which contains a workbook called EXC271. He opens the workbook and then saves it as PROFIT to his personal storage location.

The PROFIT report, which is the car dealer's own abbreviation for a Performance Review of Finance and Insurance Totals, summarizes the number of new and used cars that are sold in a given month, including the number of financing, insurance, warranty, and rust protection packages. After reviewing the worksheet, Scott decides to make a few additions and modifications.

- In cell A1, edit the title to read "Profitability Review of Finance and Insurance Totals."
- In cells G3 and H3, enter the headings "Total Cars" and "Revenue," respectively.
- In cell G5, enter a formula that adds the number of new car sales to the number of used car sales.
- In cell H5, enter a formula that adds the revenue for new car sales to the revenue for used car sales.
- Using the fill handle, copy the formulas in cells G5 and H5 down their respective columns to row 9.
- Using the AutoSum feature, sum the values in columns C through H and place the results in row 10.

Save the workbook and keep it open for use in the next problem.

2. Wednesday morning does not start out well for Scott. The owner of the dealership calls to request that Granby Insurance no longer track the sale of "Rust Protection" packages. He also asks Scott to hide the "Used Car" columns in the report. Fortunately, Scott remembers how to remove and hide cells, rows, and columns. He also feels that this is a great opportunity to adjust some of the worksheet's column widths and row heights. Specifically, Scott performs the following steps:

- Select the "best fit" or "AutoFit" width for column A. Notice that the width is adjusted to handle the length of the title in cell A1.
- Specify a column width of 18 characters for column A.
- Specify a column width of 9 characters for columns C through H.
- Specify a row height of 7.50 points for row 4.
- Ensure that column B is empty. Then delete the entire column.
- Select the cell range (A8:G8) for Rust Protection. Then choose the Edit, Delete command to remove the cells from the worksheet and shift the remaining cells upward.
- Select columns D and E. Then hide the columns from displaying.

Your screen should now appear similar to Figure 2.17. Save the workbook and keep it open for use in the next problem.

Figure 2.17

Manipulating columns and rows in a worksheet

	A	B	C	F	G	H
1	Profitability Review of Finance and Insurance Totals					
2						
3	Product Category	New Cars	Revenue	Total Cars	Revenue	
4						
5	Retail Sales	20	492,000	35	630,000	
6	Life Ins. Policies	4	1,250	6	3,750	
7	Option Packages	5	2,150	5	2,150	
8	Ext. Warranties	1	375	2	715	
9	Totals	30	495775	48	636615	
10						

3. Scott decides that it would be helpful to develop a projection for next month's PROFIT report. Rather than create a new worksheet, he unhides columns D and E and then copies the data from cells A3 through G9 to the Windows Clipboard. He moves the cell pointer to cell A12 and then pastes the data. In order to start with a clean slate, Scott selects cells B14 through G17 and erases the cell contents in the range. Then he selects cell B14 and enters a formula that shows an increase of 20% over the value stored in cell B5. In other words, he multiplies the value in cell B5 by 1.2. Lastly, Scott copies the formula to the remaining cells in the range. The workbook appears similar to Figure 2.18. To ensure that the projection area works properly, Scott changes some of the values in the top table area. Satisfied that the bottom table area updates automatically, he saves and closes the workbook.

Figure 2.18

Creating a projection based on an existing range of cells

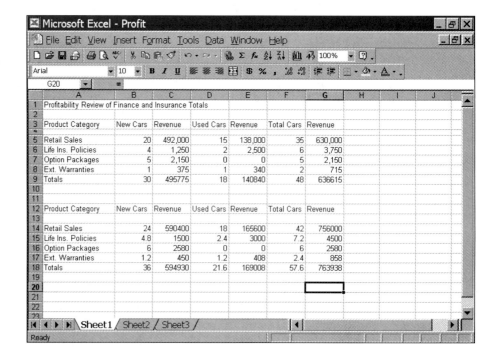

4. Scott opens a second workbook that he receives from his friend called EXC274. He then saves the workbook as "Car Buyers" to his personal storage location. This particular workbook stores customer information from each sale made in the month.

   Scott reviews the worksheet and decides to make a few changes. First, he inserts a new column A and then enters 1 into cell A4 and 2 into cell A5. Using the mouse, he selects both cells and then drags the range's fill handle downward to continue numbering the customers. *What is the number of the last customer, Heidi Buehre?* He then moves to cell E12 and displays the Auto-Complete pick list. *What vehicles are listed in the pick list and in what order do they appear?* To remove the pick list, Scott presses the ⌷ ESC ⌷ key. Lastly, Scott uses Excel's AutoCalculate feature to sum the purchase price of all vehicles sold in January without having to enter a formula into the worksheet. *What is the total value of vehicles purchased?*

   Ready to go home for the day, Scott saves and then closes the workbook. Then he exits Microsoft Excel.

Notes

MICROSOFT EXCEL 2000
Formatting and Printing

CHAPTER
THREE

Chapter Outline

3.1 Enhancing a Worksheet's Appearance

3.2 Applying and Removing Formatting

3.3 Printing and Web Publishing

3.4 Customizing Print Options

3.5 Chapter Review

3.6 Review Questions

3.7 Hands-On Projects

3.8 Case Problems

Learning Objectives

After reading this chapter, you will be able to:

- Format cell entries to appear boldface or italic and with different typefaces and font sizes

- Format numeric and date values

- Format cells to appear with borders, shading, and color

- Preview and print a worksheet

- Publish a worksheet to the World Wide Web

- Define page layout options, such as margins, headers, and footers, for printing your worksheets

Case Study   Marvin's Music

Marvin's Music is an independently owned sidewalk store that is located in the downtown core of Randall, Virginia. Established in 1974, Marvin's has successfully sold record albums, 8-track tapes, cassettes, and audio CDs. And, just recently, they began stocking movie videos and DVDs. For the past 25 years, Marvin's most prominent business strategy has been a commitment to stocking a large selection of music that appeals to a broad audience. They have always taken pride in their large inventory and in providing personalized customer service.

Stacey Marvin, the store's owner and general manager, is concerned for her business. She recently read in the newspaper that a large discount superstore is planning to move into the area. In a meeting with Justin Lee, her senior sales associate, she discussed some possible advertising ideas for combating the new competitor. For the past 18 months, Justin has been acting as Stacey's right hand. He handles much of the purchasing and receiving duties and is the primary contact person for Marvin's suppliers. Justin is also familiar with using the custom accounting software and Microsoft Excel, both of which are loaded on the office's personal computer.

In this chapter, you and Justin learn more about working with Excel worksheets. First, you learn how to format a worksheet to make it appear more attractive and easier to read. After previewing and printing a worksheet, you learn to save it as an HTML document for publishing to a Web site. Lastly, you customize several layout options, such as margins and headers, for more effective printing.

3.1 Enhancing a Worksheet's Appearance

Most people realize how important it is to create worksheets that are easy to read and pleasing to the eye. Clearly, a visually attractive worksheet will convey information better than an unformatted one. With Excel's formatting capabilities, you can enhance your worksheets for publishing online or to print. In addition to choosing from a variety of fonts, styles, and cell alignments, you can specify decimal places and add currency and percentage symbols to values. The combination of these features enables you to produce professional-looking spreadsheet reports and presentations.

3.1.1 Applying Fonts, Font Styles, and Colors

FEATURE

Applying **fonts** to titles, headings, and other worksheet cells is often the most effective means for drawing a reader's attention to specific areas in your worksheet. You can also specify font styles, like boldface and italic, adjust font sizes, and select colors. Do not feel obliged, however, to use every font that is available to you in a single worksheet. Above all, your worksheets must be easy to read—too many fonts, styles, and colors are distracting. As a rule, limit your font selection for a single worksheet to two or three **typefaces**, such as Times New Roman and Arial.

METHOD

To apply character formatting, select the desired cell range and then:

- CLICK: Font list box ([Arial ▼])
- CLICK: Font Size list box ([10 ▼])
- CLICK: Bold button ([B])
- CLICK: Italic button ([I])
- CLICK: Underline button ([U])
- CLICK: Font Color button ([A ▼])

To display the *Font* formatting options:
1. SELECT: cell range to format
2. CHOOSE: Format, Cells
3. CLICK: *Font* tab in the Format Cells dialog box
4. SELECT: the desired font, font style, size, color, and effects

PRACTICE

In this lesson, you open and format a workbook that tracks a mutual fund portfolio.

Setup: Ensure that Excel is loaded.

1 Open the data file named EXC310.

2 Save the file as "My Portfolio" to your personal storage location.

3 Your first step is to select the cell range to format. Do the following to begin formatting the column labels:
SELECT: cell range from A3 to G3

4 Let's make these labels bold and appear with underlining:
CLICK: Bold button (⬛)
CLICK: Underline button (⬛)

5 Now you will format the title labels in cells A1 and A2. To begin:
SELECT: cell range from A1 to A2

6 To change the typeface used in the cells:
CLICK: down arrow attached to the Font list box (⬛Arial⬛)
Your screen should now appear similar but not identical to Figure 3.1.

Figure 3.1

Selecting a typeface from
the Font list box

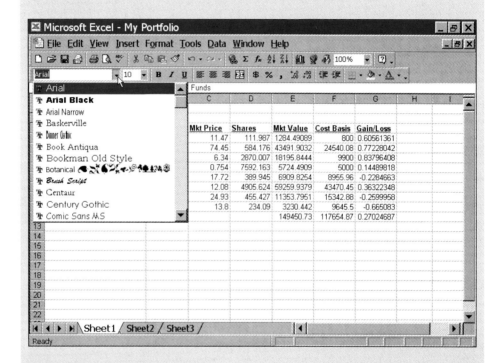

7 Using the scroll bars attached to the drop-down list box:
SELECT: Times New Roman

8 To increase the font size:
CLICK: down arrow attached to the Font Size list box (⬛10⬛)
SELECT: 14
The cells now appear formatted using a 14-point, Times New Roman typeface; the row heights have also been adjusted automatically.

9 You can also use the Format Cells dialog box to apply formatting to the selected cell range. Do the following:
SELECT: cell A1
CHOOSE: Format, Cells
CLICK: *Font* tab
Your screen should now appear similar to Figure 3.2.

Figure 3.2

Format Cells dialog

box: *Font* tab

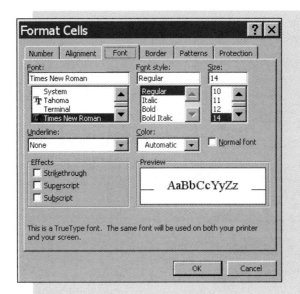

10 To add some additional flare to the title:
SELECT: *any typeface* from the *Font* list box
SELECT: Bold in the *Font style* list box
SELECT: 16 in the *Size* list box
SELECT: Blue from the *Color* drop-down list box
CLICK: OK
The title in cell A1 should now stand out from the rest of the data.

11 You can also use shortcut keys to apply formatting:
SELECT: cell range from A12 to G12
PRESS: CTRL +b to apply boldface

12 Save the workbook and keep it open for use in the next lesson.

3.1.2 Formatting Numbers and Dates

FEATURE

Numeric formats improve the appearance and readability of numbers in a worksheet by inserting dollar signs, commas, percentage symbols, and decimal places. Although a formatted number or date appears differently on the worksheet, the value that is stored and displayed in the Formula bar does not change. Excel stores date and time entries as values and, therefore, allows you to customize their display as you do numbers.

METHOD

To apply number formatting, select the desired cell range and then:

- CLICK: Currency Style button (⌷)
- CLICK: Percent Style button (⌷)
- CLICK: Comma Style button (⌷)
- CLICK: Increase Decimal button (⌷)
- CLICK: Decrease Decimal button (⌷)

To display the *Number* formatting options:

1. SELECT: cell range to format
2. CHOOSE: Format, Cells
3. CLICK: *Number* tab
4. SELECT: a number or date format from the *Category* list box
5. SELECT: formatting options for the selected category

PRACTICE

You will now apply number, currency, percentage, decimal place, and date formatting to the worksheet.

Setup: Ensure that you have completed the previous lesson and that the "My Portfolio" workbook is displayed.

1 Columns B and G in the worksheet contain data that is best represented using a percent number format. First, column B displays the proportional share of an investment compared to the total portfolio. Column G calculates the gain or loss performance. To display these calculated results as percentages, do the following:
SELECT: cell range from B4 to B11
PRESS: `CTRL` and hold it down
SELECT: cell range from G4 to G12

2 Release the `CTRL` key after the last range is selected. Notice that these two ranges are highlighted independently—ready for formatting. (*Hint*: You will no longer be reminded to release the `CTRL` key when dragging the cell pointer over a range.)

3 To apply a percent style:
CLICK: Percent Style button (⌷)

4 To display the percentages with two decimal places:
CLICK: Increase Decimal button (⌷) twice

5 Let's apply some further number formatting:
SELECT: cell range from C4 to F11
CHOOSE: Format, Cells
CLICK: *Number* tab

6 In the Format Cells dialog box that appears:
SELECT: Number in the *Category* list box
SELECT: 2 in the *Decimal places* text box
SELECT: *Use 1000 Separator (,)* check box
SELECT: Black (1,234.10) in the *Negative numbers* list box
Your screen should now appear similar to Figure 3.3.

Figure 3.3

Format Cells dialog
box: *Number* tab

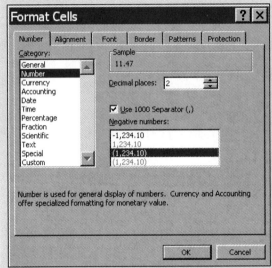

7 To apply the formatting options:
CLICK: OK

8 To increase the decimal places in the Shares column:
SELECT: cell range from D4 to D11
CLICK: Increase Decimal button (⊞)

9 To format the summary values using the Currency style:
SELECT: cell range from E12 to F12
CLICK: Currency Style button (⊞)

10 Depending on your system, the columns may not be wide
enough to display the formatted values. With the two cells still
selected:
CHOOSE: Format, Column, AutoFit Selection
You should now see all the data appearing in the column.

11 Let's develop a notes area:
SELECT: cell A14
TYPE: **Notes**
PRESS: ⬇

12 To enter the first note or comment:
TYPE: **31-Aug-99**
PRESS: ➡
TYPE: **The market rebounded from a low of 9,200 in
June.**
PRESS: **ENTER**

13 SELECT: cell A15
In the Formula bar, notice that the date reads 8/31/1999.

14 To format the date to appear differently on the worksheet:
CHOOSE: Format, Cells
Notice that "Date" is already selected in the *Category* list box and that the current date format appears highlighted in the *Type* list box.

15 To apply a new format, you select one of the listed versions:
SELECT: "March 14, 1998" in the *Type* list box
CLICK: OK command button
(*Note:* The *Type* list box displays the date formats for March 14, 1998. Keep in mind that you are selecting a display format and not a date value to insert into the worksheet.) Your screen should now appear similar to Figure 3.4.

Figure 3.4

Applying number and date formats

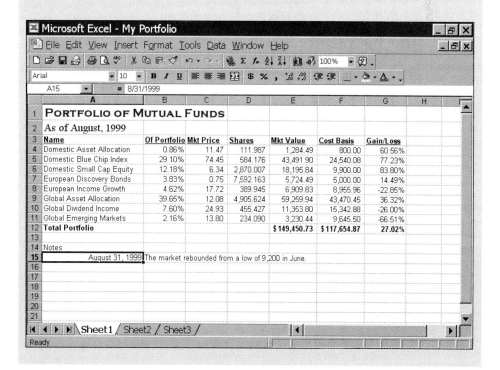

3.1.3 Aligning and Merging Cells

FEATURE

You can change the **cell alignment** for any type of data entered into a worksheet. By default, Excel aligns text against the left edge of a cell and values against the right edge. Not only can you change these default alignments, you can also merge or combine data across cells.

METHOD

To align and merge data, select the desired cell range and then:

● CLICK: Align Left button (▤)
● CLICK: Center button (▤)
● CLICK: Align Right button (▤)
● CLICK: Merge and Center button (▦)

To display the *Alignment* formatting options:

1. SELECT: cell range to format
2. CHOOSE: Format, Cells
3. CLICK: *Alignment* tab
4. SELECT: to align or merge cells

PRACTICE

You will now practice aligning cell information and merging cells.

Setup: Ensure that you have completed the previous lessons in the module and that the "My Portfolio" workbook is displayed.

1　You align the contents of a cell using buttons on the Formatting toolbar. Let's manipulate the "Notes" title in cell A14:
SELECT: cell A14
CLICK: Bold button (▣)
CLICK: Underline button (▣)

2　To practice changing a cell's alignment:
CLICK: Align Right button (▤)
CLICK: Align Left button (▤)
CLICK: Center button (▤)
Notice the change in alignment that takes place with each mouse click.

3　You can change the cell alignment for number and date values also:
SELECT: cell A15
CLICK: Center button (▤)
The date appears centered under the column heading for "Notes."

4　A little more interesting is the ability to merge cells together and center the contents. Do the following:
SELECT: cell range from A1 to G1
CLICK: Merge and Center button (▦)
Notice that the title is now centered over the table area. (*Note:* The merged cell is considered cell A1. The next cell in the row is cell H1.)

5 Let's merge and center the subtitle in cell A2 using the dialog box:
SELECT: cell range from A2 to G2
CHOOSE: Format, Cells
CLICK: *Alignment* tab
Your screen should now appear similar to Figure 3.5.

Figure 3.5

Format Cells dialog box: *Alignment* tab

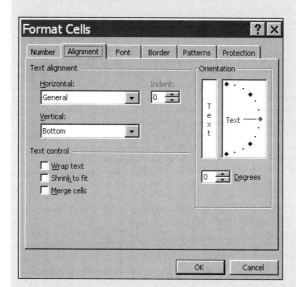

6 In the Format Cells dialog box:
SELECT: Center from the *Horizontal* drop-down list box
SELECT: *Merge cells* check box
CLICK: OK command button

7 Let's practice splitting up a merged cell without using the Undo command:
SELECT: cell A2 (which now covers the area to G2)
CHOOSE: Format, Cells
The last tab that was selected in the dialog box (*Alignment*) is displayed automatically.

8 To remove the merged cell:
SELECT: *Merge cells* check box so that no "✔" appears
CLICK: OK command button
The entry remains centered, but only between column A's borders.

9 Save the workbook and keep it open for use in the next lesson.

3.1.4 Adding Borders and Shading

FEATURE
As with the other formatting options, you use borders, patterns, shading, and colors to enhance a worksheet's readability. The gridlines that appear in the worksheet window are nonprinting lines, provided only to help you line up information. Borders can be used to place printed gridlines on a worksheet and to separate data into logical sections. These formatting options also enable you to create professional-looking invoice forms, memos, and tables.

METHOD
To apply borders or coloring, select the desired cell range and then:
● CLICK: Borders button (▦)
● CLICK: Fill Color button (▦)

To display the Border and Patterns formatting options:
1. SELECT: cell range to format
2. CHOOSE: Format, Cells
3. CLICK: *Border* or *Patterns* tab
4. SELECT: borders or pattern, shading, and fill color options

PRACTICE
In this exercise, you further format the worksheet by applying borders and fill coloring to selected cell ranges.

Setup: Ensure that you have completed the previous lessons in the module and that the "My Portfolio" workbook is displayed.

1 In order to better see the borders that you will apply in this lesson, let's remove the **gridlines** from the worksheet display:
CHOOSE: Tools, Options
CLICK: *View* tab
SELECT: *Gridlines* check box, so that no check mark appears
CLICK: OK

2 Now let's apply some borders:
SELECT: cell range from A12 to G12
CLICK: down arrow attached to the Borders button (▦)
A drop-down list of border options appears, as shown on the next page.

3 From the drop-down list that appears:
SELECT: Top and Double Bottom Border button (▦)
CLICK: cell A1 to remove the highlighting
A nice border now separates the data from the summary information. You may have noticed that clicking the Underline button (⊔) underlines only the words in a cell, while applying borders underlines the entire cell.

4 Let's apply a new fill color (sometimes called *shading*) to emphasize the title in cell A1:
CLICK: down arrow attached to the Fill Color button (▥▾)
A drop-down list of colors appears, as shown below.

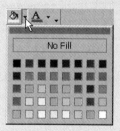

5 SELECT: a dark blue color from the drop-down list
The title should now appear on a colored background.

6 To see the title, you need to adjust the text color:
CLICK: down arrow attached to the Font Color button (▲▾)
SELECT: white from the drop-down list
Your screen should now appear similar to Figure 3.6.

Figure 3.6

Applying borders and
colors to a worksheet

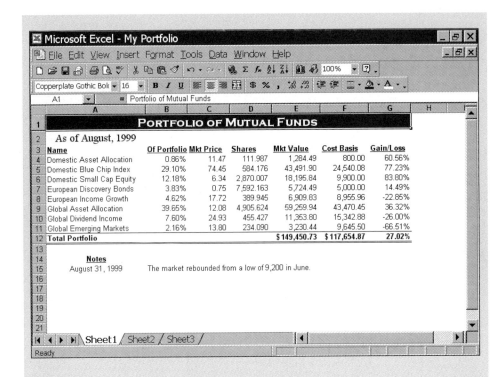

  7 To turn the worksheet gridlines back on:
CHOOSE: Tools, Options
CLICK: *View* tab
SELECT: *Gridlines* check box, so that a "✔" appears
CLICK: OK

8 On your own, apply a border underline and a light gray shading
(fill color) to the cell range A2 to G2. You can see how a subtle
use of color can produce a truly professional-looking worksheet.

9 Save and then close the workbook.

3.1 Self Check   What is the basic difference between using the Underline button (🅄)
and the Borders button (▦)?

3.2 Applying and Removing Formatting

Excel 2000 provides a wealth of formatting commands for improving
the appearance of a worksheet, its individual cells, and the contents
within those cells. In addition to selecting formatting options indi-
vidually, you can use the Format Painter button (✐) and the Edit,
Paste Special command to copy formatting characteristics. These
tools, along with Excel's AutoFormat feature, can help you apply

EXCEL

formatting commands to a worksheet consistently and more efficiently. In this module, you work with these tools as well as learn how to remove formatting characteristics from a worksheet.

3.2.1 Using Format Painter

FEATURE
You use the **Format Painter** feature to copy formatting styles and attributes from one area in your worksheet to another. Not only does this feature speed formatting procedures, it ensures formatting consistency among cells in your worksheet.

METHOD
To copy formatting from one cell range to another:
1. SELECT: the cell range whose formatting you want to copy
2. CLICK: Format Painter button (🖌) on the Standard toolbar
3. SELECT: the cell range that you want to format

PRACTICE
You will now use Format Painter to copy formatting from one area of a worksheet to another.

Setup: Ensure that no workbooks are open in the application window.

1 Open the data file named EXC320.

2 Save the file as "ABC Retailers" to your personal storage location.

3 You will now apply formatting commands to the first journal entry in the worksheet. Then, once the formatting is completed, you will copy the set of formatting options to the other journal entries. To begin:
SELECT: cell A5

4 To change the date formatting:
CHOOSE: Format, Cells
CLICK: *Number* tab
SELECT: Date in the *Category* list box
SELECT: 3/14/1998 in the *Type* list box
CLICK: OK command button
The cell entry now appears as 10/10/1999.

5 To emphasize the account numbers and explanation:
SELECT: cell range from C5 to C6
CLICK: Bold button (B)
SELECT: cell B7
CLICK: Italic button (I)
SELECT: Green from the Font Color button (A)

6 To show the values in the Amount column as currency:
SELECT: cell range from D5 to E6
CLICK: Currency Style button ($)
CLICK: Decrease Decimal button ( ) twice
The journal entry now appears formatted. (*Hint:* If necessary, increase the width of columns D and E to display the currency values.)

7 Using Format Painter, you will copy the formatting from this journal entry to another journal entry in the worksheet. Do the following:
SELECT: cell range from A5 to E7

8 To copy the formatting attributes:
CLICK: Format Painter button ( ) on the Standard toolbar
Notice that a dashed marquee appears around the selected range.

9 To apply the formatting to the next journal entry:
CLICK: cell A9
Notice that you need only click the top left-hand cell in the target range. Your screen should now appear similar to Figure 3.7.

Figure 3.7

Applying a formatting coat
using Format Painter

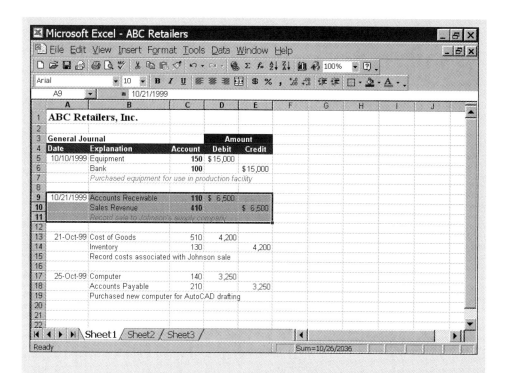

10 You can apply more than one coat using Format Painter. To demonstrate, ensure that the cell range A9 through E11 remains highlighted and then do the following:
DOUBLE-CLICK: Format Painter button (🖌)
Double-clicking the toolbar button will make the button stay active even after you apply the first coat to a target cell range.

11 With the Format Painter button (🖌) toggled on, you can apply multiple formatting coats. Do the following:
CLICK: cell A13
CLICK: cell A17
The remaining journal entries have been formatted.

12 To toggle this feature off:
CLICK: Format Painter button (🖌)

13 To better view your handiwork, do the following:
PRESS: CTRL + HOME

14 Save the workbook and keep it open for use in the next lesson.

3.2.2   Removing Formatting Attributes

FEATURE
You can safely remove a cell's formatting without affecting the contents of the cell. The easiest method, of course, is to click the Undo button (⌐⌐) immediately after choosing a formatting command. You can also remove formatting characteristics by choosing the Edit, Clear, Formats command.

METHOD
To remove all formatting from a cell range:
1.   SELECT: the desired cell range
2.   CHOOSE: Edit, Clear, Formats

PRACTICE
You will now practice removing formatting characteristics from a cell range.

Setup: Ensure that you have completed the previous lessons in the module and that the "ABC Retailers" workbook is displayed.

1   Let's demonstrate the effects of entering data into a formatted cell. In this example, you will attempt to enter a value into a cell that is formatted to display a date. Do the following:
SELECT: cell A17
TYPE: **1000**
PRESS: [ENTER]
The cell displays 9/26/1902.

2   You will now remove the formatting from this cell:
SELECT: cell A17
CHOOSE: Edit, Clear, Formats
The cell now displays the correct value, 1000.

3   The Edit, Clear, Formats command removes all formatting from a cell or cell range. To remove a single formatting characteristic, you can simply modify that characteristic. You will now remove the green color from the journal entry's explanatory note. To do so:
SELECT: cell B19
CLICK: down arrow attached to the Font Color button (△⌐)
SELECT: Automatic from the drop-down list
The text retains the italic formatting but changes to the default black color.

4 To remove all of the formatting characteristics for the last two journal entries, do the following:
SELECT: cell range from A13 to E19
CHOOSE: Edit, Clear, Formats
Notice that the date in cell A13 is actually stored as a value, 36454. In the next lesson, you will reapply formatting to the journal entries.

3.2.3 Using the Paste Special Command

FEATURE
The Edit, Paste Special command allows you to copy portions or characteristics of a cell or cell range to another area. Some of these characteristics include cell values, formulas, comments, and formats. Like the Format Painter feature, this command is useful for copying formatting options from one cell range to another.

METHOD
To copy and paste formatting characteristics:
1. SELECT: the cell whose formatting you want to copy
2. CLICK: Copy button ()
3. SELECT: the cells where you want to apply the formatting
4. CHOOSE: Edit, Paste Special
5. SELECT: *Formats* option button
6. CLICK: OK command button

PRACTICE
In this exercise, you practice copying and pasting formatting characteristics using the Edit, Paste Special command.

Setup: Ensure that you have completed the previous lessons in the module and that the "ABC Retailers" workbook is displayed.

1 In order to paste formatting characteristics, you must first copy them to the Clipboard. Do the following:
SELECT: cell range from A9 to E11
CLICK: Copy button ()
A dashed marquee appears around the selected range.

2 To display the Paste Special dialog box:
SELECT: cell A13
CHOOSE: Edit, Paste Special
The dialog box shown in Figure 3.8 is displayed. (*Note:* There are several intermediate and advanced features accessible from this dialog box. For now, you need only focus on the *Formats* option button.)

Figure 3.8

The Paste Special dialog box

To find out more about the features of this dialog box, click the question mark button and then click on one of the option buttons. A brief ToolTip will appear. Click again to remove the ToolTip.

3 To paste the formatting:
SELECT: *Formats* option button
CLICK: OK
The formatting is applied.

4 To format the last journal entry:
SELECT: cell A17
CHOOSE: Edit, Paste Special
SELECT: *Formats* option button
CLICK: OK

5 Save and then close the workbook.

EXCEL

3.2.4 Using the AutoFormat Command

FEATURE
Rather than spend time selecting formatting options, you can use the **AutoFormat** feature to quickly apply an entire group of formatting commands to a cell range. The AutoFormat command works best when your worksheet data is organized using a table layout, with labels running down the left column and across the top row. After you specify one of the predefined table formats, Excel proceeds to apply fonts, number formats, alignments, borders, shading, and colors to the selected range. It is an excellent way to ensure consistent formatting across worksheets.

METHOD
1. SELECT: cell range to format
2. CHOOSE: Format, AutoFormat
3. SELECT: an option from the *Table format* list box

PRACTICE
You will now apply a predefined table format to a portfolio tracking worksheet.

Setup: Ensure that no workbooks are open in the application window.

1 Open the data file named EXC324.

2 Save the workbook as "Sandy's" to your personal storage location.

3 To apply an AutoFormat style to specific cells in a worksheet, select the cell range that you want to format. Do the following:
SELECT: cell range from A3 to F10
(*Hint:* As long as the table layout does not contain blank rows or columns, you can place the cell pointer anywhere in the table rather than selecting the entire range.)

4 To display the AutoFormat options:
CHOOSE: Format, AutoFormat
The AutoFormat dialog box appears as shown in Figure 3.9.

Figure 3.9

AutoFormat dialog box

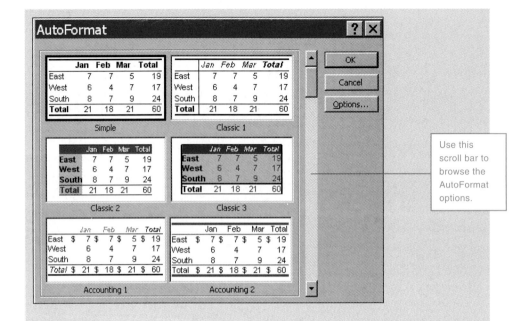

Use this scroll bar to browse the AutoFormat options.

5 After scrolling the list in the AutoFormat dialog box, do the following:
SELECT: Colorful 2 option
CLICK: OK

6 To remove the cell highlighting:
CLICK: any cell outside of the highlighted range
Your worksheet should now appear similar to Figure 3.10.

Figure 3.10

Applying an AutoFormat

	A	B	C	D	E	F	G
1	Sandy's Appliance Department						
2							
3		Qtr 1	Qtr 2	Qtr 3	Qtr 4	Total	
4	Dishwasher	5,764	6,409	6,390	7,255	25,818	
5	Dryer	8,331	12,259	10,668	10,871	42,129	
6	Microwave	2,980	3,310	1,872	2,390	10,552	
7	Refrigerator	35,400	42,810	46,230	35,788	160,228	
8	Stove/Range	24,767	28,105	27,492	21,560	101,924	
9	Washer	12,890	16,881	12,452	13,700	55,923	
10	Total	90,132	109,774	105,104	91,564	396,574	
11							
12							

7 On your own, place the cell pointer within the table area and then apply some of the other AutoFormat options, such as Classic 2.

8 Save and then close the workbook.

3.2 Self Check   How might you ensure formatting consistency among related worksheets and workbooks?

3.3 Printing and Web Publishing

This module focuses on outputting your worksheet creations. Most commonly, you will print a worksheet for inclusion into a report or other such document. However, the Internet is a strong publishing medium unto itself. With the proper access, anyone can become an author and publisher. This lesson introduces you to previewing and printing workbooks using traditional tools, but also publishing workbooks electronically on the World Wide Web.

For those of you new to the online world, the **Internet** is a vast collection of computer networks that spans the entire planet. This worldwide infrastructure is made up of many smaller networks connected by standard telephone lines, fiber optics, cable, and satellites. The term **Intranet** refers to a private and usually secure local or wide area network that uses Internet technologies to share information. To access the Internet, you need a network or modem connection that links your computer to your account on the university's network or an Independent Service Provider (ISP).

Once you are connected to the Internet, you can use Web browser software, such as Microsoft Internet Explorer or Netscape Navigator, to access the **World Wide Web**. The Web provides a visual interface for the Internet and lets you search for information by simply clicking on highlighted words and images, known as **hyperlinks**. When you click a link, you are telling your computer's Web browser to retrieve a page from a Web site and display it on your screen. Not only can you publish your workbooks on the Web, you can incorporate hyperlinks directly within a worksheet to facilitate navigating between documents.

EXCEL

3.3.1 Previewing and Printing a Worksheet

FEATURE

Before sending a worksheet to the printer, you can preview it using a full-page display that will resemble the printed version. In this Preview display mode, you can move through the workbook pages, zoom in and out on desired areas, and modify page layout options, such as margins. When satisfied with its appearance, you can send it to the printer directly.

METHOD

- To preview a workbook:
  CLICK: Print Preview button (🔍), or
  CHOOSE: File, Print Preview
- To print a workbook:
  CLICK: Print button (🖨), or
  CHOOSE: File, Print

PRACTICE

You will now open a relatively large workbook, preview it on the screen, and then send it to the printer.

Setup: Ensure that no workbooks are displayed in the application window.

1 Open the data file named EXC330.

2 Save the workbook as "Published" to your personal storage location.

3 To preview how the workbook will appear when printed:
CLICK: Print Preview button (🔍)
Your screen should now appear similar to Figure 3.11.

Figure 3.11

Previewing a workbook

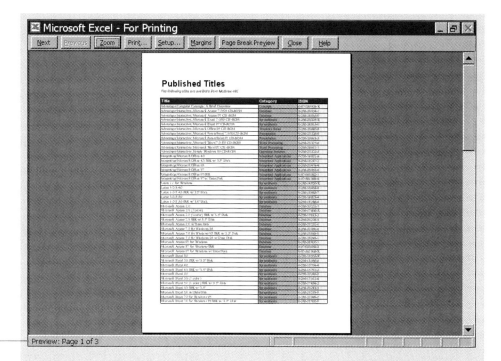

Identifies that you are in
Preview mode and viewing
"Page 1 of 3" total pages

4 To display the next page:
CLICK: Next button in the toolbar

5 To return to the first page:
CLICK: Previous button

6 To zoom in on the worksheet, move the magnifying glass mouse pointer over the worksheet area and then click once.

7 To zoom out on the display, click the mouse pointer once again.

8 On your own, practice zooming in and out on different areas of the page. You can also use the scroll bars to position the window.

10 Assuming that you are satisfied with the worksheet:
CLICK: Print button
The dialog box displayed in Figure 3.12 appears. You can use this dialog box to specify what to print and how many copies to produce. (*Note:* The quickest method for sending the current worksheet to the printer is to click the Print button (🖶) on the Standard toolbar.)

Figure 3.12

Print dialog box

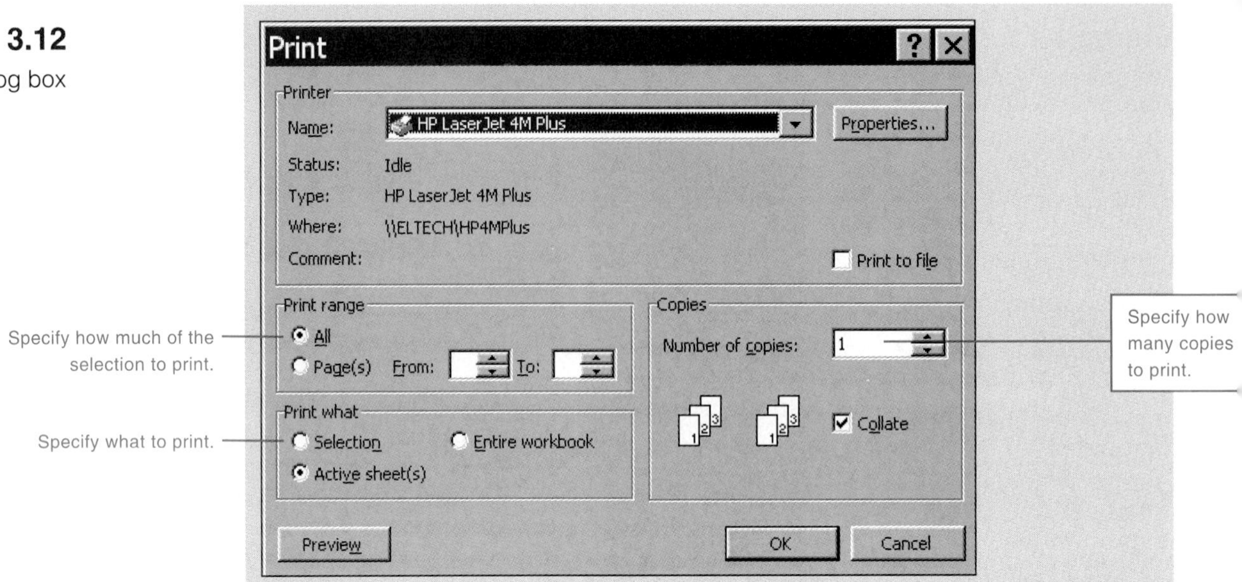

Specify how much of the selection to print.

Specify what to print.

Specify how many copies to print.

10 If you do not have access to a printer, click the Cancel button and proceed to the next lesson. If you have a printer connected to your computer and want to print out the worksheet, do the following:
CLICK: OK
After a few moments, the worksheet will appear at the printer.

3.3.2 Previewing and Publishing to the Web

FEATURE
Excel makes it easy to convert a workbook for display on the World Wide Web. The process involves saving the workbook in **HTML** (Hypertext Markup Language) format for publishing to a Web server. You can choose to publish a single worksheet or an entire workbook, complete with graphics and hyperlink objects. Once saved using the proper format, you may upload the files to your company's intranet or to a Web server.

METHOD
- To save a worksheet as a Web page:
  CHOOSE: File, Save as Web Page
- To view a worksheet as a Web page:
  CHOOSE: File, Web Page Preview

PRACTICE
You will now practice saving and viewing a worksheet as an HTML Web document.

Setup: Ensure that you have completed the previous lesson and that the "Published" workbook is displayed.

1 To save the current worksheet as a Web page:
CHOOSE: File, Save as Web Page
The Save As dialog box appears with some additional options, as shown in Figure 3.13. Notice that "Web Page" appears as the file type in the *Save as type* drop-down list box.

Figure 3.13

Save As dialog box
for a Web page

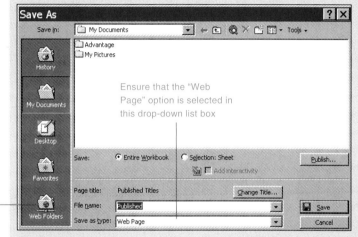

Save the Web page
directly to a Web
server on the Internet.

2 Using the *Save in* drop-down list box or the Places bar:
SELECT: *your storage location*, if not already selected
(*Note:* To publish or post your workbook Web page to an intranet or to the Internet, you can click the Web Folders button (🌐) in the Places bar and then select a server location.)

3 To proceed with the conversion to HTML:
CLICK: Save command button
The workbook document is saved as "Published.htm" to your personal storage location.

4 To preview how the workbook will appear in a Web browser:
CHOOSE: File, Web Page Preview
After a few moments, the workbook appears displayed in a Web browser window. Figure 3.14 shows the document displayed using Internet Explorer.

Figure 3.14

Viewing a worksheet
as a Web page

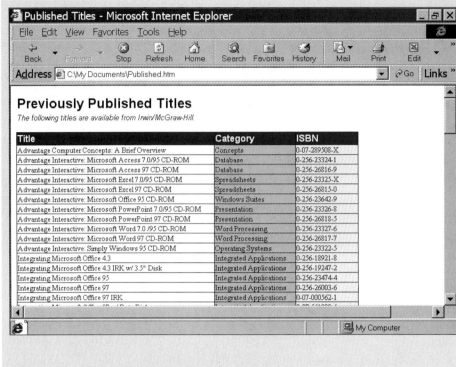

 To close the Web browser window:
CLICK: its Close button ([x])

6 Close the "Published" workbook without saving the changes.

3.3 Self Check   How does the Print Preview display mode differ from the Web Page Preview display mode?

3.4 Customizing Print Options

To assume control over how your workbooks will appear when printed, you define page layout settings using the File, Page Setup command. In the dialog box that appears, you may specify **margins, headers, footers,** and whether gridlines or row and column headings should appear on the final printed output. To make the process more manageable, Excel organizes the page layout settings under four tabs (*Page, Margins, Header/Footer,* and *Sheet*) in the Page Setup dialog box. The features and settings accessible from these tabs are discussed in the following lessons.

EXCEL

3.4.1 Adjusting Page and Margin Settings

FEATURE

You use the *Page* tab in the Page Setup dialog box to specify the paper size, print scale, and print orientation (for example, portrait or landscape) for a workbook. The *Margins* tab allows you to select the top, bottom, left, and right page margins, and to center the worksheet both horizontally and vertically on a page. You can also manipulate the page margins while viewing a worksheet in Print Preview mode.

METHOD

1. CHOOSE: File, Page Setup
2. CLICK: *Page* and *Margins* tabs
3. SELECT: the desired page layout options

PRACTICE

In this lesson, you open and print a workbook that summarizes a company's amortization expense.

Setup: Ensure that no workbooks are open in the application window.

1 Open the data file named EXC340.

2 Save the file as "CCA Schedule" to your personal storage location.

3 To begin, let's display the worksheet using Print Preview mode:
CLICK: Print Preview button ([Q])

4 Practice zooming in and out on the worksheet using the Zoom command button and the magnifying glass mouse pointer.

5 To view the second page of the printout:
CLICK: Next command button
Notice that the worksheet does not fit for printing on a single page.

6 To exit from Print Preview mode:
CLICK: Close button

7 Let's adjust some page layout settings. Do the following:
CHOOSE: File, Page Setup
CLICK: *Page* tab
Your screen should now appear similar to Figure 3.15.

Figure 3.15

Page Setup dialog

box: *Page* tab

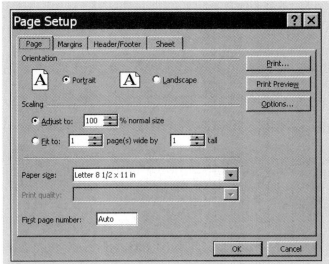

8 In the *Orientation* area:
SELECT: *Landscape* option button

9 To center the worksheet between the left and right margins:
CLICK: *Margins* tab

10 In the *Center on page* area:
SELECT: *Horizontally* check box
CLICK: Print Preview command button
You should now see the entire worksheet appear on a single
printed page and centered between the margins.

3.4.2 Inserting Headers and Footers

FEATURE
You can place descriptive information, such as the current date, in
the header and footer of a page. The contents of a header or footer
repeat automatically for each page that is printed. Some suggestions include using these areas for displaying your name, copyright
information, the words "confidential" or "first draft," or page numbering. You may simply want to place the workbook's filename in
the header so that you can easily find it again on your hard disk.

METHOD
1. CHOOSE: File, Page Setup
2. CLICK: *Headers/Footers* tab
3. SELECT: a predefined header or footer, or
    CLICK: Custom Header button to design a new header, or
    CLICK: Custom Footer button to design a new footer

PRACTICE

You will now add a custom header and footer to the worksheet.

Setup: Ensure that you have completed the previous lesson and that the "CCA Schedule" workbook is displayed in Print Preview mode.

1 To return to the Page Setup dialog box from Print Preview mode:
CLICK: Setup command button
The dialog box appears displaying the last tab that was selected.

2 To add headers and footers to the page:
CLICK: *Header/Footer* tab

3 First, select an existing footer for printing at the bottom of each page:
CLICK: down arrow attached to the *Footer* drop-down list
SELECT: "CCA Schedule, Page 1" option
Once selected, you should see the workbook's filename "CCA Schedule" appear centered in the footer preview area, and the words "Page 1" appear right-aligned.

4 To create a custom header:
CLICK: Custom Header command button
Figure 3.16 shows the Header dialog box and labels the buttons used for inserting information into the different sections.

Figure 3.16

Custom Header
dialog box

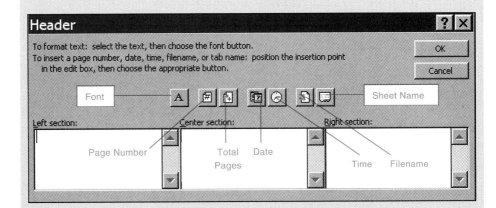

5 To create a header that prints the current date against the right margin:
CLICK: the mouse pointer in the *Right section* area
TYPE: **Printed on:**
PRESS: Space bar once
CLICK: Date button (▣) as labeled in Figure 3.16
CLICK: OK
You will see the custom header appear in the preview area.

6 To return to Print Preview mode:
CLICK: OK
Your screen should now appear similar to Figure 3.17. Notice the header in the top right-hand corner and the footer along the bottom.

7 To exit from Print Preview mode:
CLICK: Close button

Figure 3.17

Previewing the CCA Schedule worksheet

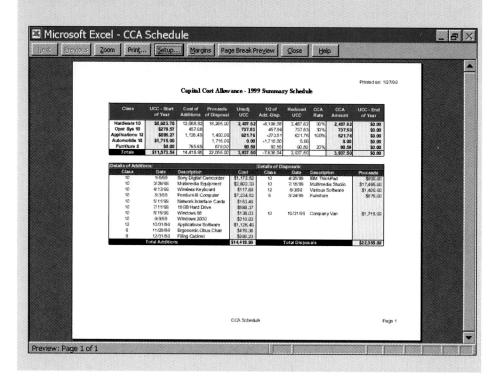

3.4.3 Selecting Worksheet Content to Print

FEATURE

From the Print dialog box, you can choose to print an entire workbook, a single worksheet, or a specified cell range. Alternatively, you can preselect a cell range to print by first specifying the print area. Other print options are available from the Page Setup dialog box, where you can choose to print the worksheet gridlines or row and column headings.

METHOD
To specify a print area:
1. SELECT: a cell range
2. CHOOSE: File, Print Area, Set Print Area

To select from the general print options:
1. CHOOSE: File, Print
2. SELECT: one of the following *Print what* option buttons—
   Selection, *Active Sheet(s)*, or *Entire Workbook*
3. SELECT: *Number of copies* to print

To specify whether to print gridlines or row and column headings:
1. CHOOSE: File, Page Setup
2. CLICK: *Sheet* tab
3. SELECT: *Gridlines* check box to toggle the printing of gridlines
4. SELECT: *Row and column headings* check box to print the
   frame area

PRACTICE
In this lesson, you practice selecting print options and setting print
areas. Lastly, you have the opportunity to print the worksheet.

Setup: Ensure that you have completed the previous lesson and that
the "CCA Schedule" workbook is displayed.

1 You will often find the need to print specific ranges in a worksheet, rather than the entire workbook. This need is solved by
first setting a print area. To practice selecting a cell range for
printing:
SELECT: cell range from A1 (a merged cell) to J12
CHOOSE: File, Print Area, Set Print Area

2 Now that you have defined a specific cell range as the print area:
CLICK: Print Preview button (⬚)
Notice that only the selected range is previewed for printing.

3 To return to the worksheet:
CLICK: Close command button

4 To return to printing the entire worksheet:
CHOOSE: File, Print Area, Clear Print Area
This command removes the print area definition.

5 Let's view some other print options:
CHOOSE: File, Page Setup
CLICK: *Sheet* tab
Your screen should now appear similar to Figure 3.18.

Figure 3.18

Page Setup dialog
box: *Sheet* tab

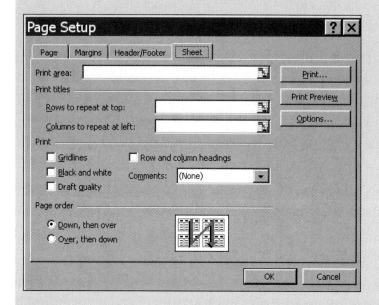

6 Sometimes printing the gridlines or row and column headings is useful for reviewing a worksheet for errors. To demonstrate:
SELECT: *Gridlines* check box in the *Print* area
SELECT: *Row and column headings* check box
CLICK: Print Preview
The printed worksheet now looks similar to the screen display, with the exception of the header and footer. (*Note:* All page setup options are saved along with the workbook file.)

7 If you have a printer connected to your computer, perform the following steps. Otherwise, proceed to the next step.
CLICK: Print command button
CLICK: OK, when the Print dialog box appears

8 If necessary, close the Print Preview window. Then save and close the "CCA Schedule" workbook.

9 Exit Microsoft Excel.

In Addition
Sending the Screen to
the Printer

Did you know that you can capture a screen image using the Print Screen or **PRTSCR** key on your keyboard? When you press **PRTSCR**, the current screen image is copied to the Windows Clipboard. You can then paste this image into a document or workbook for printing.

3.4 Self Check   How would you create a custom footer that displayed your name against the left page border and your company's name against the right page border?

3.5 Chapter Review

The majority of this chapter described common methods for enhancing the appearance of your worksheets. You were introduced to several of Excel's formatting capabilities and commands. Specifically, you applied fonts, number formats, cell alignments, borders, colors, and predefined table formats to a worksheet. You also learned how to print and electronically publish your worksheets for printing and display on the World Wide Web. Lastly, you were introduced to several of Excel's page layout options for controlling and customizing how a worksheet prints.

3.5.1 Command Summary

Many of the commands and procedures appearing in this chapter are summarized in the following table.

Skill Set	To Perform This Task . . .	Do the Following . . .
Formatting Worksheets	Apply font typefaces, font sizes, and font styles	CHOOSE: Format, Cells CLICK: *Font* tab
	Apply number formats	CHOOSE: Format, Cells CLICK: *Number* tab
	Increase and decrease decimal places	CLICK: Increase Decimal button (⊞) CLICK: Decrease Decimal button (⊞)
	Modify a cell's alignment	CHOOSE: Format, Cells CLICK: *Alignment* tab
	Merge a range of cells	CHOOSE: Format, Cells CLICK: *Alignment* tab SELECT: *Merge cells* check box

Continued

Skill Set	To Perform This Task . . .	Do the Following . . .
	Add borders, patterns, and shading	CHOOSE: Format, Cells CLICK: *Border* or *Patterns* tab
	Copy formatting from one range to another using the toolbar	SELECT: the desired range CLICK: Format Painter button (🖋) SELECT: the target range
	Copy formatting from one range to another using the Clipboard	SELECT: the desired range CLICK: Copy button (📋) SELECT: the target range CHOOSE: Edit, Paste Special SELECT: *Formats* option button
	Clear formatting that appears in a range	SELECT: the desired range CHOOSE: Edit, Clear, Formats
	Use AutoFormats	CHOOSE: Format, AutoFormat SELECT: *a predefined format*
Page Setup and Printing	Preview a worksheet	CLICK: Preview button (🔍), or CHOOSE: File, Print Preview
	Print a worksheet	CLICK: Print button (🖨), or CHOOSE: File, Print
	Preview worksheet as a Web page	CHOOSE: File, Web Page Preview
	Print the selected cell range, active worksheet, or the entire workbook	CHOOSE: File, Print SELECT: *the desired option button*
	Set the worksheet area to print workbook	SELECT: the desired range CHOOSE: File, Print Area, Set Print Area
	Clear the selected print area	CHOOSE: File, Print Area, Clear Print Area
	Specify page orientation and paper size	CHOOSE: File, Page Setup CLICK: *Page* tab
	Specify print margins and placement on a page	CHOOSE: File, Page Setup CLICK: *Margins* tab

Continued

EXCEL

Skill Set	To Perform This Task . . .	Do the Following . . .
	Define headers and footers for printing	CHOOSE: File, Page Setup CLICK: *Header/Footer* tab
	Print the screen	PRESS: PRTSCR key
Managing Files	Save worksheet as an HTML document	CHOOSE: File, Save as Web Page

3.5.2 Key Terms

This section specifies page references for the key terms identified in this chapter. For a complete list of definitions, refer to the Glossary provided in the Appendix.

AutoFormat, *p. 119*   HTML, *p. 124*

cell alignment, *p. 107*   hyperlinks, *p. 121*

fonts, *p. 102*   Internet, *p. 121*

footers, *p. 126*   Intranet, *p. 121*

Format Painter, *p. 113*   margins, *p. 126*

gridlines, *p. 110*   typefaces, *p. 102*

headers, *p. 126*   World Wide Web, *p. 121*

3.6   Review Questions

3.6.1 Short Answer

1. Why should you limit the number of typefaces used in a worksheet?
2. Name two methods for specifying decimal places in a worksheet.
3. How do you split a merged cell?
4. How do you apply multiple coats using the Format Painter tool?
5. Name two color settings that you can change in a worksheet.

6. How do you turn off gridlines from displaying in a worksheet?
7. How do you turn on gridlines for printing on a worksheet?
8. What should you do prior to sending a worksheet to the printer?
9. Name the tabs in the Page Setup dialog box.
10. How do you create a Web document from a standard Excel worksheet?

3.6.2 True/False

1. _____ The 🄱 button stands for bold. The 🅄 button stands for underline. The 🄸 button stands for incline.
2. _____ You use the *Number* tab in the Format Cells dialog box to select date and time formatting options.
3. _____ Whenever you merge cells, the contents must also be centered.
4. _____ You can remove formatting from a cell range by choosing the Edit, Clear, Special command.
5. _____ The AutoFormat command works best when your data is organized using a table layout.
6. _____ You can zoom in and out on a worksheet using Print Preview mode.
7. _____ You can view a worksheet as it would appear in a Web browser, prior to saving it as a Web page.
8. _____ The two page orientation options are *Picture* and *Land-scape*.
9. _____ You can access the Page Setup dialog box directly from Print Preview mode.
10. _____ To convert a worksheet for display on the World Wide Web, you save the workbook into HTML format.

EXCEL

3.6.3 Multiple Choice

1. To change the text color of a cell entry:
   a. CLICK: Fill Color button (▨▾)
   b. CLICK: Font Color button (▲▾)
   c. CLICK: Text Color button (▨)
   d. You cannot change the text color of a cell entry.

2. Excel stores date and time entries as:
   a. formats
   b. formulas
   c. labels
   d. values

3. To merge a range of cells, you select the *Merge cells* check box on this tab of the Format Cells dialog box:
   a. *Number* tab
   b. *Alignment* tab
   c. *Margins* tab
   d. *Merge* tab

4. To remove a cell's formatting, you can:
   a. CHOOSE: Edit, Clear, Formats
   b. CHOOSE: Edit, Formats, Clear
   c. CHOOSE: Format, Cells, Clear
   d. CHOOSE: Format, Clear

5. To copy a cell's formatting characteristics to another cell, you can:
   a. Use the AutoFormat feature
   b. Use the AutoPainter feature
   c. Use the Format Painter feature
   d. Use the Edit, Paste Formats command

6. To select one of Excel's prebuilt table formats:
   a. CHOOSE: Format, AutoTable
   b. CHOOSE: Format, TableFormat
   c. CHOOSE: Format, AutoFormat
   d. CHOOSE: Format, Table

7. To produce gridlines on your printed worksheet:
   a. SELECT: *Gridlines* check box in the Page Setup dialog box
   b. CLICK: Gridline button (▦▾) on the Formatting toolbar
   c. CLICK: Underline button (𝐮) on the Formatting toolbar
   d. Both a and b above

8. To identify a specific cell range on the worksheet for printing:
   a. CHOOSE: File, Print Range
   b. CHOOSE: File, Print Area, Set Print Area
   c. CHOOSE: File, Set Print Area
   d. CHOOSE: File, Set Print Range

9. To print data at the top of each page, you create the following:
   a. footer
   b. footnote
   c. headline
   d. header

10. To save the current worksheet as a Web page:
    a. CLICK: Save button ()
    b. CHOOSE: File, Save as Web Page
    c. CHOOSE: File, Save as HTML
    d. CHOOSE: File, Publish to Web

3.7 Hands-On Projects

3.7.1 Grandview College: Bookstore Inventory

In this exercise, you practice using Excel's formatting commands to enhance the appearance of a monthly bookstore report.

1. Load Microsoft Excel.
2. Open the data file named EXC371.
3. Save the workbook as "Bookstore" to your personal storage location.
4. Let's start by formatting the worksheet's title:
   SELECT: cell A1
   CHOOSE: Format, Cells
   CLICK: *Font* tab in the dialog box
5. In the Format Cells dialog box, make the following selections:
   SELECT: Times New Roman in the *Font* list box
   SELECT: Bold Italic in the *Font style* list box
   SELECT: 16 in the *Size* list box
   SELECT: Dark Red in the *Color* drop-down list box
   Notice that the *Preview* area in the dialog box displays all of your choices.

6. To accept the dialog box selections:
    CLICK: OK
7. Let's center the title across the width of the worksheet:
    SELECT: cell range from A1 to G1
    CLICK: Merge and Center button (⊞)
8. To apply percentage formatting:
    SELECT: cell range from D4 to D9
    CLICK: Percent Style button (%)
    CLICK: Increase Decimal button (⫶⁰⁰) twice
9. To apply currency formatting:
    SELECT: cell range from C4 to C10
    CLICK: Currency Style button ($)
    (*Hint:* You include cell C10 in the range so that you can later copy this column's formatting to other ranges in the worksheet.)
10. Let's copy this column's formatting to the other columns. With the range still selected, do the following:
    DOUBLE-CLICK: Format Painter button (◌̸)
    CLICK: cell E4 to apply one formatting coat
    CLICK: cell G4 to apply another formatting coat
    CLICK: Format Painter button (◌̸) to toggle the feature off
    (*Note:* Don't bother changing the column widths just yet.)
11. Now apply an AutoFormat to the data area:
    SELECT: cell range from A3 to G10
    CHOOSE: Format, AutoFormat

12. In the AutoFormat dialog box:
    SELECT: Classic 2
    CLICK: OK
13. To better see the results of the formatting:
    CLICK: cell A1
    A much nicer looking report!
14. Save and then close the workbook.

3.7.2 Fast Forward Video: Sales Analysis

You will now practice enhancing the layout of an existing worksheet by adjusting rows and columns and by formatting its text labels, numbers, and headings.

1. Open the data file named EXC372.
2. Save the workbook as "Video Sales" to your personal storage location.
3. To begin, adjust the width of column C to 5 characters:
   SELECT: cell C1
   CHOOSE: Format, Column, Width
   TYPE: **5**
   CLICK: OK
4. Now, delete row 3 using the following steps:
   RIGHT-CLICK: row 3 in the frame area
   CHOOSE: Delete
5. To format the headings:
   SELECT: cell A4
   PRESS: [CTRL] and hold it down
   CLICK: cell A9
   CLICK: Bold button ([B])
   Remember to release the [CTRL] key when you are finished.
6. To format the "Total Sales" label with boldface and italic:
   SELECT: cell A14
   CLICK: Bold button ([B])
   CLICK: Italic button ([I])
7. To format the two column headings:
   SELECT: cell range from D3 to E3
   PRESS: [CTRL]+b to apply boldface
   PRESS: [CTRL]+u to underline the contents
8. To format the values in the Amount column:
   CLICK: cell D5
   PRESS: [SHIFT] and hold it down
   CLICK: cell D14
   All of the cells between these two should now appear highlighted.
9. To apply currency formatting:
   CLICK: Currency Style button ([$])
10. To apply percent formatting to the values in the adjacent column:
    SELECT: cell range from E5 to E12
    CLICK: Percent Style button ([%])
    CLICK: Increase Decimal button ([.0]) twice

EXCEL

11. To format all of the category labels at the same time:
SELECT: cell range from B5 to B8
PRESS: (CTRL) and hold it down
SELECT: cell range from B10 to B12 by dragging with the mouse
There should now be two highlighted ranges on the worksheet.
12. To italicize the data and align it to the right:
CLICK: Italic button (𝐼)
CLICK: Align Right button (▤)
13. Finally, let's format the titles in rows 1 and 2. Do the following:
SELECT: cell range from A1 to A2
CLICK: Bold button (𝐁)
CLICK: down arrow attached to the Font list box (Arial ▾)
SELECT: Times New Roman
CLICK: down arrow attached to the Font Size list box (10 ▾)
SELECT: 14
14. To center the titles across the active area:
SELECT: cell range from A1 to E1
CLICK: Merge and Center button (▦)
SELECT: cell range from A2 to E2
CLICK: Merge and Center button (▦)
Your worksheet should now appear similar to Figure 3.19.
15. Save and then close the workbook.

Figure 3.19

Formatting the Sales Analysis worksheet

	A	B	C	D	E	F
1			Fast Forward Video			
2			Sales Analysis			
3				Amount	Pct of Total	
4	Rentals					
5		New Releases		$1,071.35	43.79%	
6		Weekly Movies		$ 826.00	33.76%	
7		Games		$ 549.10	22.44%	
8		Total Rentals		$2,446.45	84.63%	
9	Retail Sales					
10		Videos		$ 132.50	29.83%	
11		Snacks		$ 311.65	70.17%	
12		Total Retail		$ 444.15	15.37%	
13						
14	Total Sales			$2,890.60		
15						

3.7.3 Sun Valley Frozen Foods: Inventory Projections

Incorporating some skills learned in Chapter 2, you will now practice modifying a worksheet and applying formatting commands.

1. Open the workbook named EXC373.
2. Save the workbook as "Sun Seasonal" to your personal storage location.
3. Adjust the width of column A to 18 characters.
4. Delete column B.
5. Adjust columns B through E to their best-fit widths.
6. Format the headings in row 1 to appear boldface and centered in their respective columns.
7. Format the "Total" label in cell A7 to appear boldface and italic.
8. Insert two rows at the top of the worksheet for entering a title. (*Hint:* Rather than performing the Insert command twice to insert two rows, you can select rows 1 and 2 first and then perform the command once.)
9. Enter a title for the worksheet:
   SELECT: cell A1
   TYPE: Seasonal Inventory Projections
   PRESS: ENTER
10. Merge and center the title in cell A1 between columns A and E.
11. Format the title to appear with a larger and more unique font. Also, apply a dark blue color to the font text on a light yellow background fill. Then, surround the merged cell with a Thick Box border.
12. To bring out the Total row, apply a Top and Double Bottom border to cells A9 through E9. With the cell range highlighted, assign a light gray background fill color.

13. To remove the highlighting:
    CLICK: cell A1
14. Save and then close the workbook.

■ 3.7.4 Lakeside Realty: Listing Summary

In this exercise, you use the AutoFormat command and modify the page layout in an existing workbook.

1. Open the workbook named EXC374.
2. Save the workbook as "Listing Summary" to your personal storage location.
3. Apply the "Classic 3" AutoFormat style to the cell range from A3 to K10.

4. PRESS: HOME to remove the highlighting
5. Format the worksheet title in cell A1 to make it stand out from the table information.
6. Use the Page Setup dialog box to change the page orientation to *Landscape*.
7. Use the Page Setup dialog box to center the worksheet horizontally on the page.
8. Add a footer that prints the workbook's filename aligned left and the page number aligned right.
9. Add a header that shows the company name, "Lakeside Realty," aligned left and the current date aligned right.
10. Preview the worksheet. Your screen should now appear similar to Figure 3.20.

Figure 3.20

Previewing a
formatted worksheet

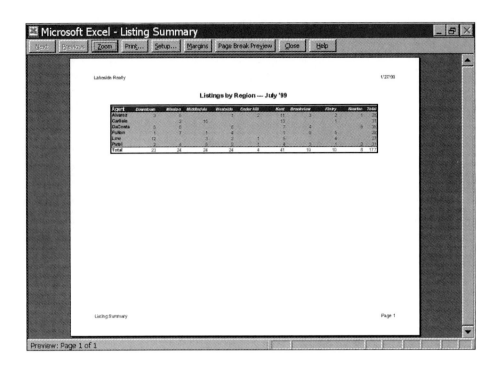

11.   Print a copy of the worksheet.
12.   Save and then close the workbook.

3.7.5 On Your Own: Financial Data Table

To practice formatting and manipulating data, open the workbook named EXC375. Then make a copy of the file by saving the workbook as "Financial Data" to your personal storage location. On your own, resize all of the columns to ensure that the data is visible. Insert a new row at the beginning of the worksheet and enter the worksheet title "United Consolidated Group." Using fonts, colors, alignment, and background fills, format the titles in rows 1 and 2 to stand out from the rest of the data.

Format the data in columns B through D with currency formatting and two decimal places, except for the date headings. Format the data in column E with percent formatting and two decimal places. Center and apply boldface to the column headings in row 3. Then apply boldface and italics to the cell range from A4 to A9. Before proceeding, adjust the column widths and row heights as required. When satisfied, preview and print the worksheet. Lastly, save and then close the workbook.

3.7.6 On Your Own: Personal Expense Comparison

To practice working with formatting and page layout options, use Excel to create a monthly expense comparison worksheet. After displaying a blank workbook, enter the following column headings in a single row: **Expense**, **January**, **February**, and **Change**. Then enter the following expense categories in a single column under the "Expense" heading.

- Rent/Mortgage
- Food
- Clothing
- Transportation
- Utilities
- Education
- Entertainment

For both the January and February columns, enter some reasonable data. Add the label "Total" below the last expense category and then use AutoSum to calculate totals for the monthly columns. Create formulas to calculate the difference for each expense category. Lastly, use the AutoFormat "Accounting 2" option to format the worksheet.

For printing purposes, add a custom footer that prints the current date, your name, and the page number at the bottom of each page. When you are finished, save the workbook as "My Expenses" to your personal storage location. Preview and print the worksheet, and then close the workbook and exit Excel.

3.8 Case Problems: Marvin's Music

Marvin's Music store is facing increased competitive pressures with the recent announcement that a discount superstore chain is moving into the area. Stacey Marvin realizes that in order to stay competitive, she needs to be able to track and analyze her inventory costs, stock levels, and sales trends quickly and accurately. Fortunately, her senior sales associate, Justin Lee, has explained how he can use Excel to create worksheets that will make these tasks easier.

In the following case problems, assume the role of Justin and perform the same steps that he identifies. You may want to re-read the chapter opening before proceeding.

1. Stacey asks Justin to prepare a worksheet that will summarize Marvin's current stock levels. He begins by launching Microsoft Excel so that a new blank workbook is displayed. As shown in Figure 3.21, he enters the worksheet title, row and column labels, and inventory values for each category.

Figure 3.21

Creating an inventory worksheet

	A	B	C	D	E
1	Inventory by Category				
2		CDs	Tapes	Total	
3	Pop	18500	6500		
4	Rock	23600	15350		
5	Dance	19000	9200		
6	Country	15420	8670		
7	Easy Listening	11330	3200		
8	Classical	5680	1340		
9	Soundtracks	4200	1030		
10	Total				
11					

Using the AutoSum feature, Justin has Excel calculate totals for both the row and column values. He then selects the cell range from A2 to D10 and applies the "Classic 2" AutoFormat style. Not yet satisfied, he merges and centers the title between columns A and D, and then applies formatting to make it appear consistent with the rest of the worksheet. Justin saves the workbook as "MM Inventory1" to his *personal storage location* and then prints a copy to show to Stacey.

2. After reviewing the worksheet, Stacey asks Justin to make the following adjustments:

- Insert a new row for "World Music" at row 9, enter 4100 for CDs and 3500 for Tapes, and ensure the totals are updated.
- Adjust the width of column A to 15 characters and then change the height of row 1 to 24 points.
- Make the values appear with dollar signs and commas, but with no decimal places.
- Adjust the width of columns B, C, and D to be larger than they presently appear and ensure that they are all the same width.

When Justin finishes customizing the worksheet to appear similar to Figure 3.22, he saves the workbook as "MM Inventory2" to the same location.

Figure 3.22

Customizing the
inventory worksheet

	A	B	C	D	E
1	Inventory by Category				
2		CDs	Tapes	Total	
3	Pop	$18,500	$6,500	$25,000	
4	Rock	$23,600	$15,350	$38,950	
5	Dance	$19,000	$9,200	$28,200	
6	Country	$15,420	$8,670	$24,090	
7	Easy Listening	$11,330	$3,200	$14,530	
8	Classical	$5,680	$1,340	$7,020	
9	World Music	$4,100	$3,500	$7,600	
10	Soundtracks	$4,200	$1,030	$5,230	
11	Total	$101,830	$48,790	$150,620	
12					

3. The next day, Stacey assigns Justin the task of completing the company's Advertising Schedule worksheet that she started a few days earlier. Justin opens the workbook named EXC383 and then saves it as "MM Ad Schedule" to his *personal storage location*. According to the sticky notes attached to Stacey's printout of the worksheet, Justin needs to enter the following three new promotions:

    Back-to-School—1 newspaper ad on August 27th for $500
    Rocktober Blitz—6 radio spots on October 11th for $2900
    Christmas—3 TV ads starting Dec 1st for $9000

    Using the toolbar, Justin formats the worksheet by applying the Currency style to the "Cost" column and then decreases the decimal places shown to 0. He adjusts the width of column F to show all of the information displayed. Then he uses the Format Cells dialog box to change the date values to appear using a "dd-mmm-yy" format. Again, he adjusts the column width as necessary.

    Noticing that Stacey placed an extra column between the "Theme" and "Date" columns, Justin deletes column B and then resizes column A to display using its best-fit width. He also selects a new typeface and font size for the column headings, and modifies the alignment of the titles. Justin prints, saves, and then closes the workbook.

4. Having completed his work for Stacey, Justin opens one of his pet worksheet projects named EXC384. This workbook contains a sales transaction analysis that summarizes information from the store's point-of-sale equipment. He immediately saves the workbook as "MM Daily Sales" to his *personal storage location*.

To speed the formatting process, Justin uses the AutoFormat feature to apply a combination of table formatting attributes to the worksheet. Then, to distinguish the cells containing the times of day from the rest of the worksheet area, Justin applies a dark red fill color to the background of row 1 and makes the font color white. Next he increases the width for all of the columns to give the worksheet a more spacious look. At the top of the worksheet, Justin inserts a new row and then enters the title "Sales Transactions by Time Period." He merges and centers the title over the columns and then applies formatting to make the title stand out from the data.

To prepare for printing, Justin adds a custom header that places the company name at the center of the page. He then adds a custom footer that contains the words "Prepared by *your name*" on the right, the date in the center, and the page number on the right-hand side. Next, he adjusts the page setup so the worksheet is centered horizontally on the page. Justin then saves the workbook as a Web page and views it using his Web browser. Satisfied that he's put in a full day, Justin saves and closes the workbook. Then he exits Microsoft Excel.

MICROSOFT EXCEL 2000
Analyzing Your Data

CHAPTER
FOUR

Chapter Outline

4.1   Working with Named Ranges

4.2   Using Built-In Functions

4.3   Creating an Embedded Chart

4.4   Chapter Review

4.5   Review Questions

4.6   Hands-On Projects

4.7   Case Problems

Learning Objectives

After reading this chapter, you will be able to:

- Create, modify, remove, and apply range names

- Understand absolute and relative cell addresses

- Use natural language formulas in a worksheet

- Use mathematical and statistical functions, such as SUM, AVERAGE, COUNT, MIN, and MAX

- Use date functions, such as NOW and TODAY

- Embed, move, and size a chart on a worksheet

- Preview and print a chart

EXCEL

Case Study

Interior Hockey Association

The Interior Hockey Association consists of eight junior hockey teams in as many communities. The IHA is run by a small group of dedicated volunteers who handle everything from coaching to administration. An ex-player himself, Brad Stafford has volunteered for the organization for the past four years. In addition to fundraising, Brad is responsible for keeping records and tracking results for all of the teams in the league.

Shortly after the end of the season, the IHA publishes a newsletter that provides various statistics and other pertinent information about the season. In the past, this newsletter required weeks of performing manual calculations, followed by days of typing results into a word processor. Having enrolled in an Excel course last month, Brad now realizes that worksheets and charts can help him to complete his upcoming tasks.

In this chapter, you and Brad learn about using ranges and functions in Excel worksheets. First, you use named ranges to create formula expressions that are easier to understand. Then you practice using Excel's built-in functions to perform calculations. Lastly, you learn how to plot and print your worksheet data in a chart.

4.1 Working with Named Ranges

In its simplest form, a cell range is a single cell, such as B4. Still, the term *cell range* is more commonly used to describe a "from here to there" area on a worksheet. A range can also cover a three-dimensional area, crossing more than one worksheet within a workbook. In a new workbook, Excel provides three worksheets named *Sheet1, Sheet2,* and *Sheet3.* It may help you to think of a worksheet as a tear-off page on a notepad—the notepad representing the workbook. You access the worksheets in a workbook by clicking on the tabs appearing along the bottom of the document window.

A **range name** is a nickname given to a group of cells that can later be used in constructing formulas. For example, the formula expression =**Revenue-Expenses** is far easier to understand than =**C5-C6**. Working with cell references from more than one worksheet adds another level of complexity. For example, if the value for Revenue is stored on Sheet1 and the value for Expenses is stored on Sheet2, the formula would read =**Sheet1!C5-Sheet2!C6**. Notice that the worksheet name is separated from the cell address using an exclamation point (!). By default, range names already contain this information, making them far easier to remember than these cryptic expressions.

In this module, you learn how to name ranges and how to work with different types of cell references.

4.1.1 Naming Cell Ranges

FEATURE
By naming parts of a worksheet, you make it (and the formulas contained therein) much easier to read and construct. There are two ways to name cell ranges. First, click in the Name box, located at the far left of the Formula bar, and then type a unique name with no spaces. Second, use a menu command to create names automatically from the row and column headings appearing in a worksheet.

METHOD
To name a cell range using the Name box:
1. SELECT: the desired range
2. CLICK: in the Name box
3. TYPE: *a range name*

To name a cell range using the Menu bar:
1. SELECT: the desired range, including the row and column headings
2. CHOOSE: Insert, Name, Create

PRACTICE
You will now name cell ranges appearing in an existing worksheet using the two methods described above.

Setup: Ensure that Excel is loaded

1 Open the data file named EXC410.

2 Save the workbook as "Salaries" to your personal storage location.

3 To increase Matthew's salary by the growth factor appearing in cell B3, perform the following steps:
SELECT: cell C6
TYPE: =b6*(1+b3)
PRESS: ENTER
The answer, 41400, appears in cell C6. In order for another user to understand this calculation, they would need to track down each cell address in the formula.

4 A better approach is to name the cells that you often refer to in formulas. Let's name the cell containing the growth factor before entering a formula to increase Jennifer's salary:
SELECT: cell B3
CLICK: in the Name box with the I-beam mouse pointer
TYPE: Growth (as shown below)

Type the desired range name in the Name box.

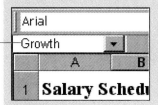

5 PRESS: ENTER
You have now created a named range called "Growth" that you can use in place of the cell address when entering formulas.

6 To use the range name:
SELECT: cell C7
TYPE: =b7*(1+Growth)
PRESS: ENTER
The answer, 53820, appears. A new user reading this formula would now be able to decipher its objective.

7 You can also use range names to navigate within your worksheet:
CLICK: down arrow attached to the Name box
SELECT: Growth in the drop-down list that appears
The cell pointer moves immediately to cell B3.

8 Now update the growth factor:
TYPE: 5%
PRESS: ENTER
The worksheet cells containing formulas are updated.

9 Another method for creating range names uses the existing heading labels in your worksheet. You can use this method effectively when the data is organized in a table layout. To demonstrate:
SELECT: cell range from A5 to D9
Notice that the selected range includes the fiscal years across the top row and the employee names down the leftmost column.

10 To specify that the heading labels be used in naming the ranges:
CHOOSE: Insert, Name, Create

11 In the Create Name dialog box, ensure that the *Top row* and *Left column* check boxes appear selected as shown in Figure 4.1.

Figure 4.1

Creating range names
from worksheet values

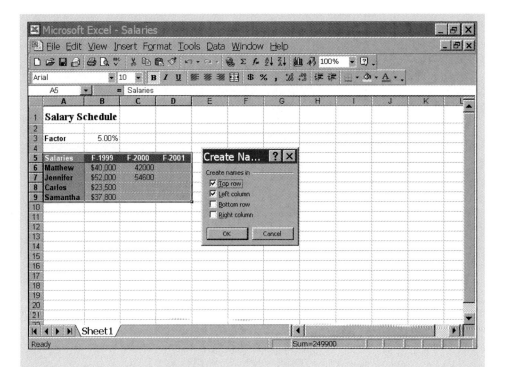

12 To complete the operation:
CLICK: OK

13 Now let's practice selecting named ranges:
CLICK: down arrow attached to the Name box
Many range names now appear in the drop-down list.

14 To move the cell pointer to one of the row ranges:
CLICK: Jennifer in the drop-down list
The cell range from B7 to D7 appears selected.

15 To display one of the column ranges:
CLICK: down arrow attached to the Name box
CLICK: F_2001 in the drop-down list
(*Note:* The label "F-2001" is used as the column heading instead
of the value 2001, since Excel can only create range names from
labels. You must also beware of conflicts with cell addresses. For
example, the range name F2001 is unacceptable because it refers
to a cell address.)

16 Lastly, let's select the entire data area in the table:
CLICK: down arrow attached to the Name box
CLICK: Salaries in the drop-down list

17 PRESS: CTRL + HOME to remove the highlighting

18 Save the workbook and keep it open for use in the next lesson.

EXCEL

4.1.2 Managing Range Names

FEATURE
Once created, you can easily modify and delete range names using the Define Name dialog box. Another useful feature is the ability to paste a list of the existing range names into your worksheet. Refer to this list when you are building formula expressions or when you need to jump to a particular spot in the worksheet.

METHOD
To display the Define Name dialog box:
• CHOOSE: Insert, Name, Define

To paste range names into the worksheet:
• CHOOSE: Insert, Name, Paste

PRACTICE
You will now practice deleting and pasting range names.

Setup: Ensure that you have completed the previous lesson and that the "Salaries" workbook is displayed.

You manipulate range names using the Define Name dialog box. To illustrate, let's delete the yearly range names that were created in the last lesson. Do the following:
CHOOSE: Insert, Name, Define
The dialog box in Figure 4.2 should now appear on the screen.

Figure 4.2

The Define Name dialog box

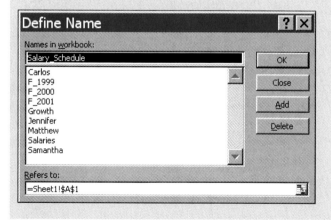

2 To remove the "F_1999" range name:
SELECT: F_1999 in the *Names in workbook* list box
Notice that the range address "=Sheet1!$B$6:$B$9" appears in the *Refer to* text box. (*Note:* If necessary, you can edit the cell references appearing in this text box. The significance of dollar signs in the range address is discussed in the next lesson.)

3 CLICK: Delete command button

4 To remove the remaining yearly range names:
SELECT: F_2000 from the list box
CLICK: Delete command button
SELECT: F_2001 from the list box
CLICK: Delete command button

5 To dismiss the dialog box:
CLICK: Close command button

6 To help you document and double-check the cell references in a worksheet, Excel enables you to paste a list of the existing named ranges into the worksheet. To demonstrate this technique:
SELECT: cell A12
CHOOSE: Insert, Name, Paste
CLICK: Paste List command button

7 To remove the highlighting:
PRESS: CTRL + HOME
Your screen should now appear similar to Figure 4.3.

8 Save the workbook and keep it open for use in the next lesson.

Figure 4.3

Pasting a list of range names into the worksheet

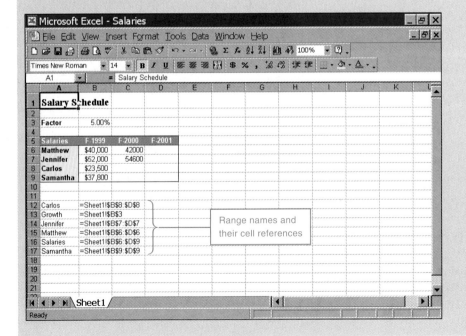

4.1.3 Using References in Formulas

FEATURE

There are two types of cell references that you can enter into formulas: *relative* and *absolute*. The difference between the two types becomes especially important when you start copying and moving formulas in your worksheet. A **relative cell address** in a formula adjusts itself automatically when copied, since the cell reference is relative to where it sits in the worksheet. An **absolute cell address** always refers to an exact cell location.

METHOD

The formulas that you have entered so far have all used relative cell references—Excel's default method. To specify an absolute reference, you precede each column letter and row number in a cell address with a dollar sign. For example, to make cell B5 an absolute cell reference, you type $B$5. A **mixed cell address,** on the other hand, locks only a portion of a cell address by placing the dollar sign ($) before either the address's column letter or row number, such as B$5. Sometimes it helps to vocalize the word "absolutely" as you read a cell address, whereby $B$5 would be read as "absolutely column B and absolutely row 5."

PRACTICE

In this lesson, you practice using relative and absolute cell addressing in performing simple copy and paste operations.

Setup: Ensure that you have completed the previous lesson and that the "Salaries" workbook is displayed.

1 Let's begin by reviewing the formula in cell C6:
SELECT: cell C6
Review the expression "=B6*(1+B3)" in the Formula bar. You can vocalize this formula as "take the value appearing to my left and then multiply it by 1 plus the value appearing three rows up and one column to the left." Notice that you need a point of reference for this formula to make any sense, which is the location of the cell pointer in cell C6.

2 Let's copy the formula in cell C6 to cell D6:
CLICK: Copy button (🖺) on the Standard toolbar
SELECT: cell D6
CLICK: Paste button (🖺)
PRESS: [ESC] to remove the dashed marquee
The result, 42000, appears in cell D6. This, however, is not the desired result. The value has not been incremented by the growth factor.

3 In the Formula bar, notice that the formula "=C6*(1+C3)" no longer performs the correct calculation. Copying and pasting has modified the cell addresses by automatically adjusting the column letters.

4 If you want to ensure that Excel does not change a cell address during a copy operation, you need to make it absolute:
PRESS: DELETE
SELECT: cell C6

5 Position the I-beam mouse pointer over the cell address B3 in the Formula bar and then click the left mouse button once.

6 To change the growth factor reference into an absolute address, you type dollar signs in front of the column letter and row number. Or, you can do the following:
PRESS: F4 ABS key (ABS stands for absolute)
Notice that B3 now appears as $B$3, as shown below.

The dollar signs in front of the column letter and row number make the cell reference absolute.

7 Continue pressing F4 to see how Excel cycles through possible combinations of relative, absolute, and mixed cell addressing.

8 Before proceeding, ensure that $B$3 appears in the Formula bar and then press ENTER.

9 Copy and paste the formula into cell D6 again. The correct result, 44100, now appears in the cell.

10 Remember that you used a range name in constructing the formula for cell C7. On your own, copy the formula in cell C7 to cell D7. Notice that the formula calculates correctly because range names, such as Growth, are defined using absolute cell addresses.

11 To continue:
PRESS: ESC to remove the marquee
PRESS: CTRL + HOME

12 Save and then close the worksheet.

4.1.4 Entering Natural Language Formulas

FEATURE
Another alternative to using cell references is to enter a special type of expression called a **natural language formula.** Similar to using range names, a natural language formula allows you to build a formula using the row and column labels from the active worksheet. In order for natural language formulas to work effectively, the worksheet should be organized using a table format with distinctly labeled rows and columns.

METHOD
1. SELECT: the cell where you want the result to appear
2. TYPE: = (an equal sign)
3. TYPE: *an expression*, using row and column labels
4. PRESS: [ENTER]

PRACTICE
You will now use natural language formulas to calculate an expression in a worksheet.

Setup: Ensure that no workbooks are open in the application window.

1 Open the data file named EXC414.

2 Save the workbook as "Natural" to your personal storage location.

3 Before you begin, you'll need to review some configuration settings:
CHOOSE: Tools, Options
CLICK: *Calculation* tab
This tab, as shown in Figure 4.4, enables you to specify calculation options and dictate whether Excel recognizes labels in formulas.

Figure 4.4

Options dialog box: *Calculation* tab

Select this option to have Excel recalculate the formulas in your worksheet whenever you change a value.

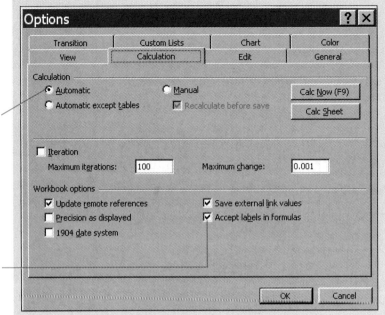

Ensure that this check box is selected before attempting to enter a natural language formula.

4 On the *Calculation* tab of the Options dialog box:
SELECT: *Automatic* option button
SELECT: *Accept labels in formulas* check box so that a "✔" appears
CLICK: OK command button

5 To calculate the profit for Q1 using a natural language formula:
SELECT: cell B6
TYPE: =**Revenue-Expenses**
PRESS: ➡
The result, 32500, appears in the cell. (*CAUTION:* You cannot mix labels with cell references in a natural language formula. For example, the formula =**Revenue-B5** does not compute.)

6 To proceed, enter the same natural language formula into cells C6, D6, and E6. Notice that Excel calculates the results correctly.

7 Save and then close the workbook.

4.1 Self Check   Why is "AD1999" an unacceptable name for a cell range?

4.2 Using Built-In Functions

This module introduces you to Excel's built-in **functions.** Don't let the word *function* conjure up visions of your last calculus class; functions are shortcuts that you use in place of entering lengthy and complicated formulas. Functions are incredible time-savers that can increase your productivity in creating worksheets.

There are several methods for entering a function into a worksheet cell. To begin with, you can type a function name, preceded by an equal sign (=), and then enter its **arguments** (labels, values, or cell references). Many functions are quite complex, however, and all require that you remember the precise order, called **syntax,** in which to enter arguments. An easier method is to select a function from the Paste Function dialog box shown in Figure 4.5. You access this dialog box by choosing the Insert, Function command or by clicking the Paste Function button ([*fx*]). In addition to organizing Excel's functions into tidy categories (further described in Table 4.1), the Paste Function dialog box lets you view a function's syntax, along with a brief description.

Figure 4.5

Paste Function
dialog box

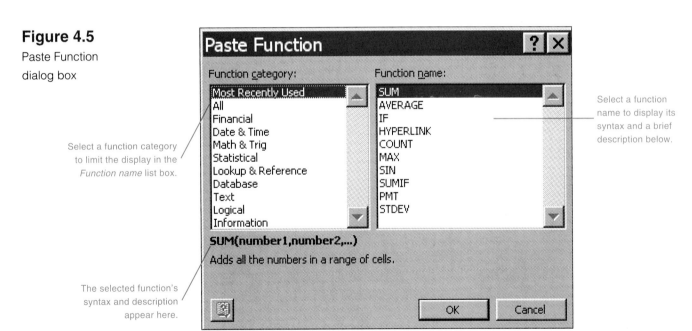

Select a function category to limit the display in the *Function name* list box.

Select a function name to display its syntax and a brief description below.

The selected function's syntax and description appear here.

Table 4.1

Function Categories

Category	Description
Financial	Determine loan payments, present and future values, depreciation schedules, and rates of return
Date & Time	Perform date and time calculations; input the current date and/or time into a cell
Math & Trig	Sum a range of values; perform trigonometric calculations; determine absolute and rounded values
Statistical	Determine the average, median, minimum, and maximum values for a range; calculate statistical measures, like variance and standard deviation
Lookup & Reference	Look up and select values from a range; return the active cell's column letter and row number
Database	Perform mathematical and statistical calculations on worksheet values in a table or list format
Text	Manipulate, compare, format, and extract textual information; convert values to text (and vice versa)
Logical	Perform conditional calculations using IF statements; compare and evaluate values
Information	Return information about the current environment; perform error-checking and troubleshooting

EXCEL

4.2.1 Adding Values (SUM)

FEATURE
You use the SUM function to add together the values appearing in a range of cells. SUM is the most frequently used function in Excel, saving you from having to enter long addition formulas such as =A1+A2+A3 . . . +A99. The AutoSum button (Σ) inserts the SUM function into a worksheet cell automatically, guessing at the range argument to use.

METHOD
=SUM(range)

PRACTICE
You will now practice entering the SUM function.

Setup: Ensure that no workbooks appear in the application window.

1 Open the data file named EXC420.

2 Save the workbook as "Functions" to your personal storage location. Your screen should now appear similar to Figure 4.6.

Figure 4.6

The "Functions" workbook

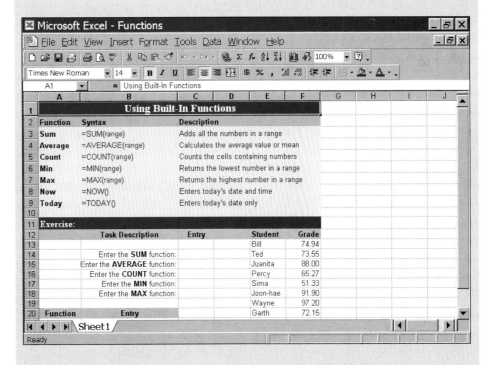

3 Let's total the grade values in column F. Do the following:
SELECT: cell C14

4 To enter the SUM function:
TYPE: =sum(f13:f22)
PRESS: ENTER
The result, 761.51, appears in the cell. (*Note:* You can enter a function's name and arguments using either lowercase or upper-case letters. Ensure that there are no blank spaces entered mistakenly.)

5 Let's change Percy's grade:
SELECT: cell F16

6 To enter the revised grade:
TYPE: 75.27
PRESS: ENTER
The new SUM result displays 771.51 in cell C14.

7 Save the workbook and keep it open for use in the next lesson.

4.2.2 Calculating Averages (AVERAGE)

FEATURE
You use the AVERAGE function to compute the average value (sometimes called the arithmetic mean) for a range of cells. This function adds together all of the numeric values in a range and then divides the sum by the number of cells used in the calculation.

METHOD
=AVERAGE(*range*)

PRACTICE
In this exercise, you calculate the average value for a named range in a worksheet.

Setup: Ensure that you have completed the previous lesson and that the "Functions" workbook is displayed.

1 To make it easier to enter functions, you can name the cell ranges on your worksheet. Let's name the range that contains the grade values:
SELECT: cell range from E12 to F22
Notice that you include the column headings, Student and Grade, in the selection.

2 CHOOSE: Insert, Name, Create

3 In the Create Name dialog box:
SELECT: *Top row* check box, if not already selected
SELECT: *Left column* check box, if not already selected
CLICK: OK command button

4 To view the range names that have been created:
CLICK: down arrow attached to the Name box
Your screen should now appear similar to Figure 4.7.

Figure 4.7

Viewing a worksheet's range names

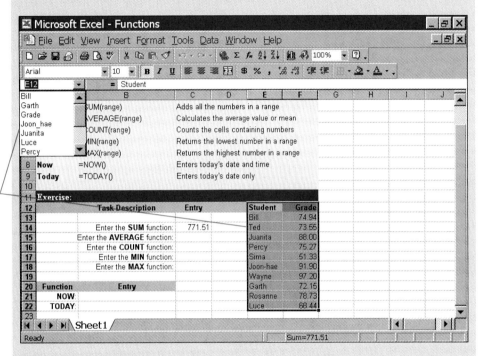

The Name Box displays the range names created from the worksheet selection.

5 In the drop-down list box that appears:
CLICK: Garth
Your cell pointer should now be positioned in cell F20. Notice also that the Name box displays the name "Garth."

6 To select the entire "Grade" range:
CLICK: down arrow attached to the Name box
CLICK: Grade in the drop-down list
The cell range from F13 to F22 is selected.

7 Let's use the range name to calculate the average grade:
SELECT: cell C15
TYPE: =average(grade)
PRESS: ENTER
The result, 77.151, appears in the cell.

8 To determine the average of a list of nonadjacent values, separate the items in the list using commas. To illustrate:
SELECT: cell D15
TYPE: `=average(Bill,Ted,Sima,Rosanne)`
PRESS: `ENTER`
The result, 69.6375, appears as the average of only these students' grades.

4.2.3 Counting Values (COUNT)

FEATURE
The COUNT function counts the number of cells in a range that contain numeric or date values. This function ignores cells containing text labels.

METHOD
`=COUNT(`*range*`)`

PRACTICE
You will now enter the COUNT function in the "Functions" workbook.

Setup: Ensure that you have completed the previous lessons and that the "Functions" workbook is displayed.

1 Move the cell pointer to where you want the result to appear:
SELECT: cell C16

2 You will now use the mouse to help you count the number of entries in a range. To begin:
TYPE: `=count(`

3 Using the mouse, position the cell pointer over cell F13. Then:
CLICK: cell F13 and hold down the left mouse button
DRAG: mouse pointer to cell F22
Notice that as you drag the mouse pointer, the range is entered into the function as an argument. When you reach cell F22, the argument displays the range name "Grade."

4 Release the mouse button.

5 To complete the function entry:
TYPE: `)`
PRESS: `ENTER`
The result, 10, appears in cell C16.

6 Save the workbook and keep it open for use in the next lesson.

4.2.4 Analyzing Values (MIN and MAX)

FEATURE
You use the MIN and MAX functions to determine the minimum (lowest) and maximum (highest) values in a range of cells.

METHOD
=MIN(*range*)
=MAX(*range*)

PRACTICE
In this lesson, you practice using the **Formula Palette** to calculate the minimum and maximum grades in a range. The Formula Palette provides a helpful dialog box for selecting and entering function arguments in the correct order.

Setup: Ensure that you have completed the previous lessons in this module and that the "Functions" workbook is displayed.

1 To calculate the lowest grade achieved:
SELECT: cell C17
TYPE: =min(grade)
PRESS: ➡
The result, 51.33, appears.

2 To find the lowest grade achieved among three students:
TYPE: =min(Wayne,Garth,Luce)
PRESS: ENTER
The result, 68.44, appears.

3 You will now use Excel's Formula Palette to calculate the maximum value in a range. Do the following:
SELECT: cell C18
TYPE: =max(
Ensure that you include the open parentheses "(" at the end of the function name.

4 To display the Formula Palette:
CLICK: Edit Formula button (=) in the Formula bar
The Formula Palette appears under the Formula bar, as shown in Figure 4.8. (*Note:* You can ignore the Assistant character that may appear on your screen. He, she, or it will go away after you complete the next few steps.)

Figure 4.8

Formula Palette:

Entering the MAX function

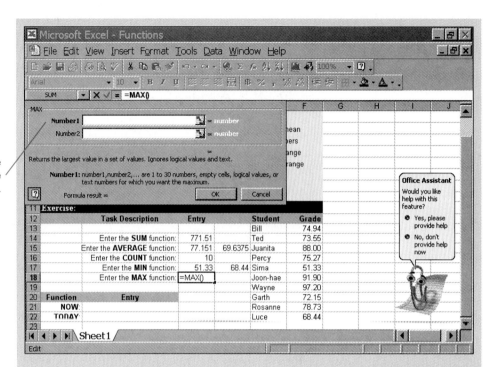

You use the Formula Palette when you need assistance entering a function.

5 In the *Number1* argument text box:
TYPE: `grade`
Notice that the actual cell contents appear at the right of the text box and that the result is calculated immediately and shown below.

6 To complete the entry:
CLICK: OK command button

7 To find the maximum grade achieved among three students:
SELECT: cell D18
TYPE: `=max(`
CLICK: Edit Formula button (☐)

8 In the Formula Palette:
TYPE: `Juanita`
PRESS: TAB
TYPE: `Ted`
PRESS: TAB
TYPE: `Luce`
Notice that the Formula bar displays the function as you build it in the Formula Palette.

9 To complete the entry:
CLICK: OK command button
The result, 88, appears in the cell.

10 Save the workbook and keep it open for use in the next lesson.

EXCEL

4.2.5 Calculating Dates (NOW and TODAY)

FEATURE

You use the NOW and TODAY functions to display the current date and time. The NOW function returns the current date and time as provided by your computer's internal clock. The TODAY function provides the current date only. Neither of these functions require any arguments.

METHOD

=NOW( )
=TODAY( )

PRACTICE

In this exercise, you insert the NOW and TODAY functions into the worksheet.

Setup: Ensure that you have completed the previous lessons in this module and that the "Functions" workbook is displayed.

1 To insert the current date and time into the worksheet, do the following:
SELECT: cell B21
TYPE: =now( )
PRESS: (ENTER)
The date is displayed using the "mm/dd/yy" format (depending on your default settings), while the time is typically displayed using the "hh:mm" 24-hour clock format.

2 To display only the time in the cell, you must format the entry:
SELECT: cell B21
CHOOSE: Format, Cells
CLICK: *Number* tab

3 You must now select a time format:
SELECT: Time in the *Category* list box
SELECT: 1:30:55 PM in the *Type* list box
CLICK: OK command button

4 To recalculate the NOW function:
PRESS: (F9) CALC key
You should see the cell value change to the current time. (*Hint:* You can use (ENTER) to recalculate all formulas and functions in a worksheet.)

5 To enter the current date only:
SELECT: B22
TYPE: =today()
PRESS: ENTER
The current date should now appear in the worksheet.

6 On your own, format the current date to display using the "14-Mar-98" format option.

7 Save and then close the workbook.

4.2 Self Check   When might you use the Formula Palette or Paste Function dialog box to enter a function into the worksheet?

4.3   Creating an Embedded Chart

Since the earliest versions of spreadsheet software, users have been able to display their numerical data using graphs and charts. While acceptable for in-house business presentations and school projects, these graphics often lacked the depth and quality required by professional users. Until now! You can confidently use Excel to produce visually stunning worksheets and charts that are suitable for electronic business presentations, color print masters, Internet Web pages, and 35mm slide shows.

There are many types of charts available for presenting your worksheet data to engineers, statisticians, business professionals, and other audiences. Some popular business charts—line chart, column chart, pie chart, and XY scatter plot diagram—are described below.

- **Line Charts**   When you need to plot trends or show changes over a period of time, the **line chart** is the perfect tool. The angles of the line reflect the degree of variation, and the distance of the line from the horizontal axis represents the amount of the variation. An example of a line chart appears in Figure 4.9, along with some basic terminology.

EXCEL

Figure 4.9

A line chart

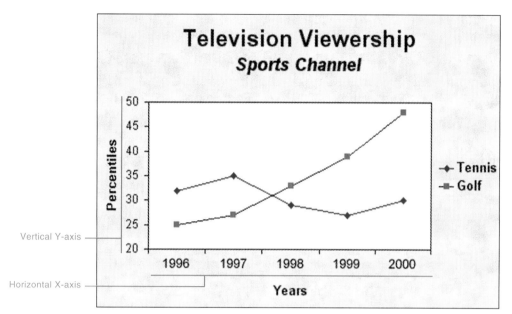

Television Viewership
Sports Channel

Vertical Y-axis

Horizontal X-axis

- *Bar or Column Charts*   When the purpose of the chart is to compare one data element with another data element, a **column chart** is the appropriate form to use. A column chart (Figure 4.10) shows variations over a period of time, similarly to a line chart. A **bar chart** also uses rectangular images, but they run horizontally rather than vertically.

Figure 4.10

A column chart

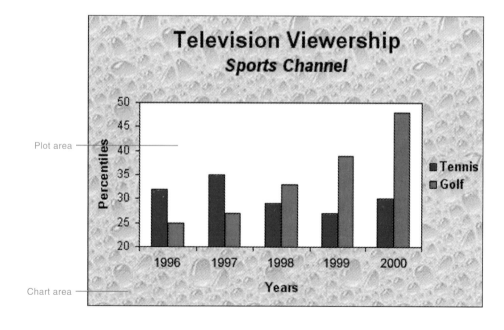

Television Viewership
Sports Channel

Plot area

Chart area

- *Pie Charts*   A **pie chart** shows the proportions of individual components compared to the total. Similar to a real pie (the baked variety), a pie chart is divided into slices or wedges. (In Excel, you can even pull out the slices from the rest of the pie.) An example of a pie chart appears in Figure 4.11.

Figure 4.11

A pie chart

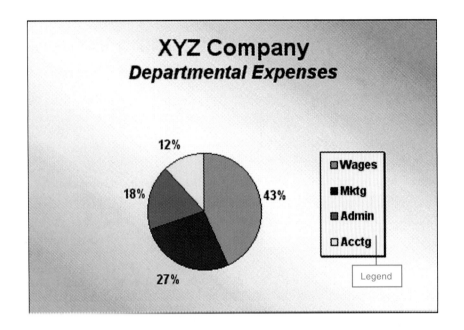

- ***Scatter Plot Charts***   **XY charts,** which are commonly referred to as *scatter plot diagrams,* show how one or more data elements relate to another data element. Although they look much like line charts, XY charts show the correlation between elements and include a numeric scale along both the X and Y axes. The XY chart in Figure 4.12 shows that worker productivity diminishes as stress levels increase.

Figure 4.12

An XY chart

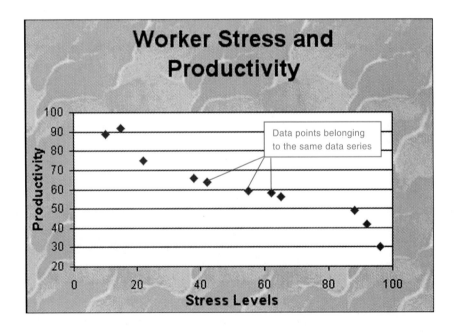

EXCEL

There are two methods for creating a chart in Excel, differing primarily in the way the chart is stored and printed. First, you can create a new chart as a separate sheet in a workbook. This method works well for printing full-page charts and for creating computer-based presentations or electronic slide shows. Second, you can create an **embedded chart** that is stored on the worksheet. Embed a chart when you want to view or print the chart alongside the worksheet data. Whichever method you choose, use the step-by-step features in Excel's **Chart Wizard** to construct a chart from existing worksheet data.

In this module, you learn how to create and print an embedded chart.

4.3.1 Creating a Chart Using the Chart Wizard

FEATURE
You create a chart by selecting a range of cells to plot and then launching the Chart Wizard. The wizard examines the selected range and then displays its dialog box. You make selections, such as choosing a chart type, and then proceed through the steps to embed the chart on the worksheet. An embedded chart is actually placed over—not entered into—a cell range. Once embedded, you can move, size, and delete the chart.

METHOD
1. SELECT: the cell range to plot in a chart
2. CLICK: Chart Wizard button (▥)
3. Complete the steps in the Chart Wizard.

PRACTICE
You will now create and embed a new chart onto a worksheet.

1 Open the data file named EXC430.

2 Save the workbook as "Cruising" to your personal storage location.

3 Let's plot the worksheet's demographic data. To begin, select both the headings and the data:
SELECT: cell range from A2 to D5

4 To start the Chart Wizard:
CLICK: Chart Wizard button (▥) on the Standard toolbar
Your screen should now appear similar to Figure 4.13. (*Note:* If the Assistant appears, right-click it and choose the Hide command.)

Figure 4.13

Chart Wizard: Step 1 of 4

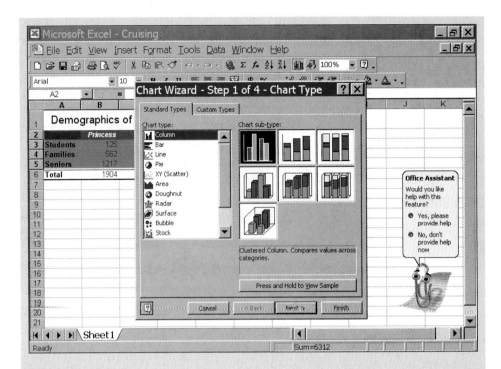

5 To see a sample of how Excel will plot this data:
CLICK: "Press and Hold to View Sample" command button
(*Note:* You must hold down the left mouse button to see the chart inside the *Sample* preview window. When finished viewing, release the mouse button.)

6 Let's select a different chart sub-type that amalgamates (adds together) the two data series in a column. Do the following:
SELECT: Stacked Column in the *Chart sub-type* area
When you click on a chart sub-type, the chart's name and description appear above the "Press and Hold to View Sample" command button.)

7 Once again, preview a sample of the chart:
CLICK: "Press and Hold to View Sample" command button

8 To continue creating the chart:
CLICK: Next> to proceed to Step 2 of 4 for selecting data
CLICK: Next> to proceed to Step 3 of 4 for selecting data

9 In Step 3 of 4 of the Chart Wizard:
TYPE: **Cruise Lines** into the *Category (X) axis* text box
TYPE: **Passengers** into the *Value (Y) axis* text box
(*Hint:* Click the I-beam mouse pointer into a text box and then type the appropriate text. You can also press **TAB** to move forward through the text boxes.) Notice that the preview area is immediately updated to display the new titles, as shown in Figure 4.14.

Figure 4.14

Chart Wizard:

Step 3 of 4

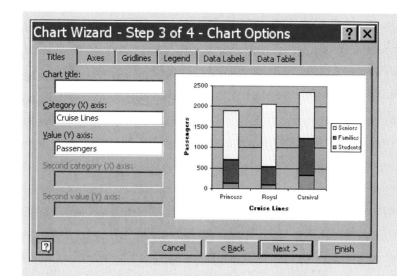

10 To proceed to the final step:
CLICK: Next >

11 In Step 4 of 4, you specify where you want to store the chart. To create an embedded chart:
SELECT: *As object in* option button, if it is not already selected
Notice that the current worksheet's name, Sheet1, already appears in the drop-down list box next to the option button.

12 To complete the Chart Wizard:
CLICK: Finish
The embedded chart appears in the application window. (*Note:* You may also see Excel's Chart toolbar appear.)

13 The black selection handles that surround the chart indicate that it is currently selected. Using the mouse, you can size the embedded chart by dragging these handles. On your own, practice sizing the chart.

14 You can also move the chart by dragging the object using the mouse. Position the white mouse arrow over a blank portion of the chart's background area. Then, drag the chart into position. Practice moving and sizing the chart to appear similar to Figure 4.15.

Figure 4.15

Moving and sizing an
embedded chart object

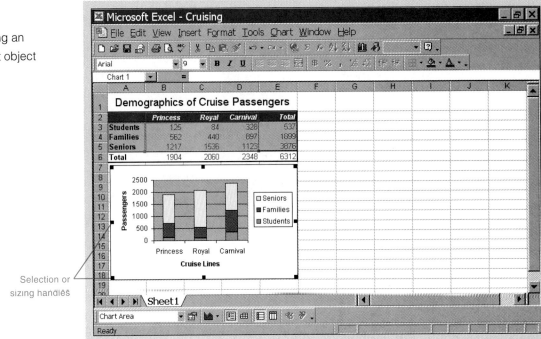

Selection or
sizing handles

15 To return focus to the worksheet:
CLICK: any visible cell in the worksheet area, such as cell F1
Notice that the Chart toolbar and the selection boxes around the
chart both disappear.

16 The embedded chart is dynamically linked to the information
stored in the worksheet. To demonstrate, let's update the "Carni-
val" column in the embedded chart:
SELECT: cell D5
TYPE: **123**
PRESS: (ENTER)
The chart is updated immediately to reflect the new data.

17 To undo the last change:
CLICK: Undo button (⟲)

18 Save the workbook and keep it open for use in the next lesson.

4.3.2 Previewing and Printing an Embedded Chart

FEATURE
One of the primary reasons for embedding a chart on a worksheet is to view and print it alongside its worksheet data. You must ensure that the print area (or range), however, includes the entire chart object. And, as before, remember to preview your worksheet and chart prior to printing.

METHOD
1. SELECT: a cell range that includes the chart
2. CHOOSE: File, Print Area, Set Print Area
3. CHOOSE: File, Print or
   CHOOSE: File, Print Preview

PRACTICE
In this lesson, you preview and print an embedded chart along with its worksheet data.

Setup: Ensure that you have completed the previous lesson and that the "Cruising" workbook is displayed.

1 To print the worksheet and embedded chart on the same page:
SELECT: cell range from A1 to F20
(*Note:* Depending on the size and placement of your chart object, you may need to increase or decrease this print range. Make sure that the entire object is covered in the highlighted range.)

2 CHOOSE: File, Print Area, Set Print Area

3 To preview the worksheet and chart:
CLICK: Print Preview button

4 To zoom in on the preview window:
CLICK: Zoom command button

5 On your own, scroll the preview window to appear similar to Figure 4.16. Notice that the chart is printed immediately and seamlessly below the worksheet data.

Figure 4.16

Previewing an embedded chart

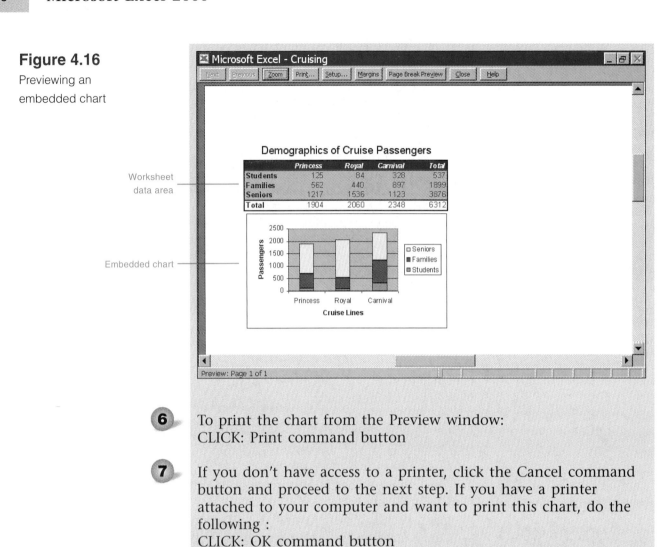

Worksheet data area

Embedded chart

6 To print the chart from the Preview window:
CLICK: Print command button

7 If you don't have access to a printer, click the Cancel command button and proceed to the next step. If you have a printer attached to your computer and want to print this chart, do the following :
CLICK: OK command button

8 To remove the highlighting from the worksheet area:
CLICK: cell A1

9 Save and then close the workbook.

10 Exit Microsoft Excel.

4.3 Self Check What must you do when selecting the print range for a worksheet that contains an embedded chart?

4.4   Chapter Review

This chapter introduced you to some powerful tools for analyzing and summarizing data. You learned how to name cells and ranges and how to use these names in constructing expressions and navigating the worksheet. The first module also discussed the differences between absolute and relative cell addresses. An absolute cell address appears with dollar signs ($), which serve to anchor an address to an exact location on the worksheet. The second module focused on Excel's built-in functions. These functions, such as SUM and AVERAGE, are used as shortcuts to performing complex or lengthy calculations. Remember to use the Formula Palette and Paste Function feature when you need assistance entering the arguments for a function. In the last module, you learned to create an embedded chart using the Chart Wizard and to position and print the chart alongside its worksheet data.

4.4.1   Command Summary

Many of the commands and procedures appearing in this chapter are summarized in the following table.

Skill Set	To Perform This Task . . .	Do the Following . . .
Working with Named Ranges	Name a cell range	SELECT: the desired range CLICK: in the Name box TYPE: *a range name*
	Create range names from labels appearing on the worksheet	SELECT: the desired range CHOOSE: Insert, Name, Create
	Modify and delete range names	CHOOSE: Insert, Name, Define
	Paste a list of range names onto the worksheet	CHOOSE: Insert, Name, Paste
Working with Formulas	Modify and use cell references (absolute, relative, and mixed)	SELECT: the desired cell CLICK: in the cell address in the Formula bar PRESS: F4 to apply reference type
	Recalculate formulas in a worksheet	PRESS: F9 CALC key

Continued

Skill Set	To Perform This Task . . .	Do the Following . . .
Using Functions	Use the Formula Palette to enter a function and its arguments	CLICK: Edit Formula button (▪)
	Insert a function using the Paste Function dialog box	CLICK: Paste Function button (*f*) SELECT: a category and function
	Use basic functions:	
	• Sum a range of values	=SUM(*range*)
	• Average a range of values	=AVERAGE(*range*)
	• Count the numeric and date values in a range	=COUNT(*range*)
	• Find the lowest value in a range	=MIN(*range*)
	• Find the highest value in a range	=MAX(*range*)
	Use date functions:	
	• Enter the current date and time	=NOW( )
	• Enter today's date	=TODAY( )
Using Charts and Objects	Use the Chart Wizard to create a chart	SELECT: the cell range to plot CLICK: Chart Wizard button (▦)
	Preview and print an embedded chart	SELECT: the desired range CHOOSE: File, Print Area, Set Print Area CLICK: Print Preview (▣) or Print (▤)

4.4.2 Key Terms

This section specifies page references for the key terms identified in this chapter. For a complete list of definitions, refer to the Glossary provided in the Appendix.

absolute cell address, *p. 157*

arguments, *p. 161*

bar chart, *p. 171*

Chart Wizard, *p. 173*

column chart, *p. 171*

embedded chart, *p. 173*

Formula Palette, *p. 167*

functions, *p. 161*

line chart, *p. 170*

mixed cell address, *p. 157*

natural language formula, *p. 159*

pie chart, *p. 171*

range name, *p. 151*

relative cell address, *p. 157*

scatter plot charts, *p. 172*

syntax, *p. 161*

XY charts, *p. 172*

4.5 Review Questions

4.5.1 Short Answer

1. Why would you want to name a range of cells?
2. How do you place a list of range names into the worksheet?
3. Name the two primary types of cell references and explain how they differ.
4. In order for natural language formulas to work effectively, how should the worksheet be organized?
5. Which function would you use to extract the highest value from a range named "salary?" How would you enter the function?
6. Which function would you use to place only the current time in your worksheet? What else might you want to do?
7. What is the name of the dialog box that you can use to select functions from categories? How do you access this dialog box?

8. What is the name of the dialog box that can help you to enter a function's arguments correctly? How do you access this dialog box?
9. Describe the four steps in creating a chart using the Chart Wizard.
10. What are the black boxes called that surround an embedded chart? What are they used for?

4.5.2 True/False

1. _____ Range names that you create use absolute cell references.
2. _____ Cell addresses that you enter into formulas use, by default, relative cell references.
3. _____ The "&s" in the cell reference &D&5 indicate an absolute cell reference.
4. _____ You cannot mix labels, such as "Revenue," with cell references in a natural language formula.
5. _____ You enter a function using parentheses instead of the equal sign.
6. _____ The SUM function appears in the Statistical function category of the Paste Function dialog box.
7. _____ You must use the Formula Palette to enter the COUNT function.
8. _____ The TODAY function updates the computer's internal clock to the current date and time.
9. _____ A pie chart shows the proportions of individual components compared to the total.
10. _____ You can move and size an embedded chart once it is placed on the worksheet.

EXCEL

4.5.3 Multiple Choice

1. What menu command allows you to create range names using the labels that already appear in the worksheet?
   a. Edit, Name, Create
   b. Range, Name, Create
   c. Insert, Name, Create
   d. Insert, Name, Define

2. Which of the following symbols precedes an absolute cell reference?
   a. $
   b. @
   c. &
   d. #

3. Which key do you press to change a cell address to being absolute, relative, or mixed?
   a. F2
   b. F3
   c. F4
   d. F9

4. Which key do you press to recalculate or update a worksheet?
   a. F2
   b. F3
   c. F4
   d. F9

5. Which is the correct expression for adding the values stored in the cell range from A1 to A20?
   a. =ADD(A1+A20)
   b. =SUM(A1:A20)
   c. =SUM(A1+A20)
   d. =AutoSUM(A1,A20)

6. Which is the correct expression for determining the average of a range named "Units"?
   a. =AVG(Units)
   b. =UNITS(Average)
   c. =AVERAGE(Units)
   d. =SUM(Units/Average)

7. What does the COUNT function actually count?
   a. All of the cells in a range
   b. All of the cells containing data in a range
   c. Only those cells containing text and numbers
   d. Only those cells containing numeric or date values

8. Which button do you click to display the Formula Palette?
   a. `=`
   b.
   c. `Σ`
   d. `ƒ*`

9. What is the name of the step-by-step charting tool provided by Excel?
   a. Chart Master
   b. Chart Wizard
   c. Plot Master
   d. Plot Wizard

10. A chart may be created as a separate chart sheet or as an embedded object. In which step of the Chart Wizard do you specify how a chart is created and stored?
    a. Step 1
    b. Step 2
    c. Step 3
    d. Step 4

4.6   Hands-On Projects

4.6.1   Grandview College: Enrollment Statistics

In this exercise, you practice creating and working with named cell ranges and constructing formulas using absolute and relative cell addresses.

1. Open the data file named EXC461.
2. Save the workbook as "Enrollment" to your personal storage location.
3. You will now name a cell range on the worksheet. To begin:
   SELECT: cell B8
   CLICK: in the Name box
   TYPE: **Total**
   PRESS: (ENTER)
   You have successfully named this cell "Total."
4. To create a set of range names using existing worksheet labels:
   SELECT: cell range from A2 to B7
   CHOOSE: Insert, Name, Create
   CLICK: OK command button
   (*Note:* The *left column* check box is selected by default in the Create Names dialog box.)

5. To view the list of range names that you just created:
   SELECT: cell E2
   CHOOSE: Insert, Name, Paste
   CLICK: Paste List command button
   SELECT: cell A1 to remove the highlighting
   (*Note:* The list is pasted in alphabetical order.)
6. To enter a formula using named cell ranges:
   SELECT: cell B10
   TYPE: =
   CLICK: cell B3
   TYPE: +
   CLICK: cell B7
   Notice that the expression "`=Continuing_Ed+Vocational`"
   appears in the Formula bar.
7. To complete the formula entry:
   PRESS: `ENTER`
8. On your own, enter a formula in cell B11 that totals the rest
   of the departments not included in the previous step.
9. Let's calculate the enrollment percentage for each department.
   Starting in cell C2, you will enter a formula that can be later
   used for copying. To do so, you need to specify an absolute
   cell reference for the Total value and a relative cell reference
   for the Arts value. To illustrate:
   SELECT: cell C2
   TYPE: `=b2/total`
   PRESS: `ENTER`
   (*Note:* A range name provides an absolute cell reference. Therefore, you cannot use the range name "Arts" in the formula
   expression.)
10. To copy the formula to the remaining departments:
    SELECT: cell C2
    DRAG: the fill handle for cell C2 to cell C8
    (*Hint:* The fill handle for a cell or cell range is the small black
    box in the bottom right-hand corner of the range selection.)
11. On your own, select the cells in the range C2:C8 and view the
    contents in the Formula bar. Notice that the relative cell refer-
    ences (B2, B3,... B8) adjust automatically. The range name
    "Total" remained absolute.
12. Save and then close the "Enrollment" workbook.

4.6.2 Fast Forward Video: Rental Category Chart

You will now practice creating a chart using Excel's Chart Wizard.

1. Open the data file named EXC462.
2. Save the workbook as "Video Chart" to your personal storage location.
3. To begin, select the cell range that contains the data for plotting:
    SELECT: cell range A3 to G5
    Notice that you did not include the "Total" row or "Total" column.
4. Launch the Chart Wizard:
    CLICK: Chart Wizard button (▥) on the Standard toolbar
5. To display the two categories, New Release and Weekly, side by side:
    SELECT: Column as the *Chart type*
    SELECT: Clustered Column as the *Chart sub-type*
    CLICK: Next > to proceed to Step 2 of 4
    CLICK: Next > to proceed to Step 3 of 4
6. On the *Titles* tab of Step 3 in the Chart Wizard:
    TYPE: **Income by Category** into the *Chart title* text box
    TYPE: **Movie Category** into the *Category (X) axis* text box
    TYPE: **Rental Income** into the *Value (Y) axis* text box
    CLICK: Next >
7. To embed the chart in the worksheet:
    SELECT: *As object in* option button, if it is not already selected
    CLICK: Finish
    The chart object appears in the middle of the application window.
8. To move the embedded chart, position the mouse pointer on an empty portion of the chart's background. Then do the following:
    DRAG: the chart below the data area
9. To size the embedded chart, position the mouse pointer over the selection handle in the bottom right-hand corner. Then:
    DRAG: the selection handle down and to the right to enlarge the chart

10. On your own, finalize the size and placement of the embedded chart so that it appears similar to Figure 4.17.

Figure 4.17

Sizing and moving an embedded chart

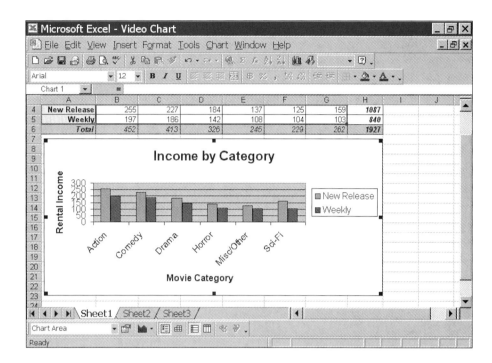

11. You've just received word that some information in the worksheet has been entered incorrectly. Study the Misc/Other category columns on the chart. Now, update the worksheet:
    SELECT: cell F4
    TYPE: **104**
    PRESS: ⬇
    TYPE: **175**
    PRESS: (ENTER)
    Notice that the chart has been updated to reflect the new values.
12. Save and then close the "Video Chart" workbook.

4.6.3 Sun Valley Frozen Foods: Daily Production

You will now practice using some of Excel's built-in functions in an existing worksheet. You will also use the AutoFill feature to create a series and then the Fill command to copy formulas.

1. Open the data file named EXC463.
2. Save the workbook as "Sun Daily" in your personal storage location.

3. Use the fill handle to complete a series listing the days of the week (Monday through Friday) in cells A3 to A7.

4. In cell B9, enter the following function to calculate the minimum production amount for corn:
TYPE: `=min(b3:b7)`
PRESS: (ENTER)

5. Using the same approach as before, enter formulas in cells B10 and B11 to calculate the maximum and average production for corn.

6. Select the cell range from B9 to E11 and then use the Edit, Fill, Right command to copy the formulas to columns C, D, and E.

7. Select the cell range from A2 to E7 and then use the Insert, Name, Create command to assign range names using the existing labels.

8. To calculate the total production for Corn:
SELECT: cell B13
TYPE: `=sum(corn)`
PRESS: (ENTER)

9. Using the same technique, calculate the totals for the Peas, Beans, and Other columns. (*Note:* You cannot use the Edit, Fill, Right command since the named range "Corn" uses an absolute cell reference.)

10. Save and then close the "Sun Daily" workbook.

4.6.4 Lakeside Realty: Mortgage Rate Chart

In this exercise, you create an embedded chart and then print it alongside the worksheet data.

1. Open the data file named EXC464.

2. Save the workbook as "Mortgage Chart" to your personal storage location.

3. Select the cell range from A2 to G8.

4. Launch the Chart Wizard.

5. In the *Chart type* and *Chart sub-type* list boxes, select a line chart with markers displayed at each data value. Then proceed to the third step.

6. In step 3 of the Chart Wizard, add the title "Average Mortgage Rates" to appear at the top of the chart. Then proceed to the next step.

7. Save the chart as an object in Sheet1 and then click the Finish command button.

8. Size and move the embedded chart so that it covers the range from cell A13 to G27.

9. Update July's six-month rate to 6.00 in the worksheet.

10. Set the print area to cover the range from A1 to H28.

11. Preview and then print the selected print area.

12. Save and then close the "Mortgage Chart" workbook.

4.6.5 On Your Own: Auto Fuel Comparison

This exercise lets you practice naming ranges and entering functions. To begin, open the EXC465 workbook and then save it as "Auto Fuel" to your personal storage location.

To begin, let's create some range names. Assign the name "Capacity" to the cell range B2:B7. Assign the name "City" to the cell range C2:C7. Assign the name "Hwy" to the cell range D2:D7. Paste a list of the range names in column F. In row 8, calculate the average for each column using their respective range names and the AVERAGE function. For more practice, enter a function in cell B10 that returns a count of the number of numerical entries in the "Capacity" range. In cell C10, display the minimum miles per gallon city rating. In cell D10, display the maximum miles per gallon highway rating.

When you are finished, save and then close the "Auto Fuel" workbook.

4.6.6 On Your Own: Personal Expense Chart

For additional practice creating charts, open the EXC466 data file. Before continuing, save the workbook as "Expense Chart" to your personal storage location. Then complete the worksheet by inputting your monthly expenses into the appropriate cells.

Using the Chart Wizard, create a pie chart of these expenses. Do not add a title to the chart and save it as an embedded object in the worksheet. Once it appears on the worksheet, size the chart so that the information is easily read. Lastly, position the chart to the right of the worksheet data. Print the worksheet data and the chart on the same page. Remember to use the Set Print Area command and Print Preview to ensure that your settings are correct. When you are satisfied with the results, send the worksheet and embedded chart to the printer.

Save and then close the "Expense Chart" workbook. Then, exit Excel.

4.7   Case Problems: Interior Hockey Association

The Interior Hockey Association is a junior hockey league that is just finishing its current season. As one of the many volunteers that keep the IHA going, Brad Stafford has the task of summarizing various statistics for inclusion into the season-end newsletter. Brad has recently learned how to use ranges and functions in Excel and now wants to use them to produce worksheets that can be incorporated into the newsletter.

In the following case problems, assume the role of Brad and perform the same steps that he identifies. You may want to re-read the chapter opening before proceeding.

1. It's 8:00 P.M. on a Sunday evening when Brad decides to sit down at his home computer and spend some time working on the IHA newsletter. After loading Excel, he opens the EXC471 workbook that he has been using to project next year's attendance levels. Brad wants to communicate the fine growth in attendance that the IHA has been experiencing. Before continuing, he saves the workbook as "IHA Attendance" to his personal storage location.

    Having learned about range names, Brad's first step is to use the Name box and apply a range name of "Factor" to cell C12. Then, he selects the cell range A2:B10 and uses the Insert, Name, Create command to create range names from the selection's row and column labels. To verify that the range names are correct, Brad selects cell E1 in the worksheet and then pastes a list of all existing named ranges.

    Brad remembers that to calculate next year's attendance using a growth factor formula, he will have to use both relative and absolute cell addresses. Otherwise, when he performs a copy operation, the formula's cell addresses will be adjusted automat-

EXCEL

ically. Brad wants to ensure that the formulas always use the value in cell C12 as the growth factor. Fortunately, Brad also remembers that a named range is, by default, an absolute reference. Therefore, using a relative cell address and the "Factor" range name, he can complete his task. To begin, he enters the formula **=b3*(1+Factor)** into cell C3. Notice that Brad typed "b3" and not "Bristol" into the cell. (*Hint:* The range name "Bristol" refers to the absolute cell address $B$3 and not the relative cell address that is required for this calculation.) This formula calculates next year's projected attendance for Bristol.

Brad uses Excel's AutoFill feature to extend the formula in cell C3 for the rest of the teams. Finally, he uses the Format Painter to copy the formatting from column B to the new results in column C. Brad saves and then closes the workbook.

2. Brad Stafford is constructing a worksheet that shows the team standings at the end of the IHA's regular season play. To review the worksheet, he opens the EXC472 file and then saves it as "IHA Standings" to his personal storage location.

   With the teams already in the proper order, Brad wants to chart their results. He selects the cell range B2:C10 and then launches the Chart Wizard. In the first step, Brad selects a "Clustered bar with a 3-D visual effect" chart. Then he clicks the Finish command button. When the embedded chart appears in the application window, Brad sizes it so that all the team names are visible on the vertical axis. He then moves the chart below row 14, as shown in Figure 4.18.

Figure 4.18

Analyzing data using an embedded chart

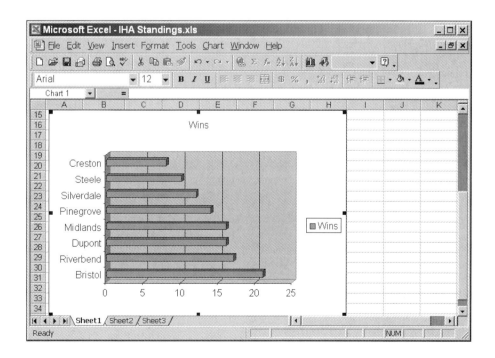

Continuing his work, Brad enters a formula into cell C12 that averages the values in that column. He uses the Fill, Right command to extend the formula across to column F. Lastly, Brad saves, prints, and then closes the workbook.

3. With the deadline for the season-end newsletter fast approaching, Brad is determined to finish the Team Goal Statistics worksheet. He opens the EXC473 data file and then saves it as "Goal Table" to his personal storage location.

   After double-checking to make sure that the formulas in column D are correct, Brad copies the formula from cell D3 to the cell range D14:D21. He then enters SUM functions into cells C11 and C22 that sum the goals for Offense and Defense, respectively. In column G, Brad uses Excel's built-in functions to find the highest, lowest, and average number of goals for both Offense and Defense. He names the two data ranges and then enters the functions into the appropriate cells. When he is finished, Brad saves and then closes the workbook.

4. The final worksheet that Brad needs to compile is for the "Scoring by Periods" statistics. He opens the EXC474 data file and saves it as "IHA Scoring" in his personal storage location.

   Using one of Excel's built-in functions, Brad calculates and displays the total goals scored by the first team in column F. After entering the function, he uses AutoFill to extend the formula to the rest of the teams. Next, he uses the appropriate function in row 11 to calculate the average for the first period. He formats the result to display using a single decimal place and then extends the formula to cover columns C through F.

   Brad completes the worksheet using the MIN and MAX functions to calculate the high and low scores for each period. As before, he extends these functions to cover the remaining columns. Lastly, Brad saves and closes the workbook and then exits Excel.

Answers to Self Check Questions

1.1 Self Check — How do you turn the adaptive menus feature on or off? Choose the Tools, Customize command and then ensure that no "✓" appears in the *Menus show recently used commands first* check box.

1.2 Self Check — Explain why a phone number is not considered a numeric value in an Excel worksheet. Although it contains numbers, a phone number is never used to perform mathematical calculations.

1.3 Self Check — Why is worksheet editing such a valuable skill? Most worksheets in use today are revisions and updates of older worksheets. As a novice user, you often spend more time updating existing worksheets than constructing new ones.

1.4 Self Check — In the Open and Save As dialog boxes, how do the List and Details views differ? What two other views are accessible from the Views button? The List view uses a multi-column format. The Details view displays one file per row. Furthermore, the Details view displays other information, including the file size, type, and modification date. The two other views are Properties and Preview.

2.1 Self Check — Which of the "Auto" features enables you to sum a range of values and display the result in the Status bar? AutoCalculate

2.2 Self Check — Which method would you use to copy several non-adjacent worksheet values for placement into a single column? The Office Clipboard would provide the fastest method. After displaying the Clipboard toolbar, you would clear the Clipboard and collect up to 12 items in the desired sequence. Then, you would move to the target range and paste these items into a single column.

2.3 Self Check — Why must you be careful when deleting rows or columns? Because if you delete the entire row or column, you may inadvertently delete data that exists further down a column or further across a row. Ensure that a row or column is indeed empty before deleting it.

3.1 Self Check — What is the basic difference between using the Underline button (U) and the Borders button (⊞)? When you apply an underline to a cell, only the words in the cell appear underlined. When you apply a border underline to a cell, the entire cell is underlined. Also, borders may be applied to each side of a cell, such as top, bottom, left, and right.

3.2 Self Check How might you ensure formatting consistency among related worksheets and workbooks? Use the same predefined AutoFormat style to format data in all of the worksheets.

3.3 Self Check How does the Print Preview display mode differ from the Web Page Preview display mode? Print Preview appears in the Excel application window and displays the workbook as it will appear when printed. Web Page Preview uses the computer's default Web browser to display an HTML rendering of the current worksheet.

3.4 Self Check How would you create a custom footer that displayed your name against the left page border and your company's name against the right page border? In the Page Setup dialog box, you would click the Custom Footer command button on the *Header/Footer* tab. Then, you would enter your name into the left text box and your company's name into the right text box of the Footer dialog box.

4.1 Self Check Why is "AD1999" an unacceptable name for a cell range? You cannot name a cell range using an actual cell reference on the worksheet.

4.2 Self Check When might you use the Formula Palette or Paste Function dialog box to enter a function into the worksheet? If you need help entering the arguments in the correct order or if you cannot remember a function's name or proper syntax, you can use these tools to refresh your memory or to assist you in completing the task.

4.3 Self Check What must you do when selecting the print range for a worksheet that contains an embedded chart? Because charts do not appear in cells on a worksheet, you must ensure to select the print range to include these graphic objects. For example, select the cells that appear underneath the embedded chart that you want to print.

Glossary

absolute cell address   Cell reference in a worksheet that does not adjust when copied to other cells. You make a cell address absolute by placing dollar signs ($) before the column letter and row number, such as $C$4.

adaptive menus   The dynamic menu bars and toolbars that are personalized to the way you work. Microsoft Office 2000 watches the tasks that you perform in an application and then displays only those commands and buttons that you use most often.

application window   In Windows, each running application program appears in its own application window. These windows may be sized and moved anywhere on the Windows desktop.

arguments   The parameters used in entering a function according to its *syntax*. Arguments may include text, numbers, formulas, functions, and cell references.

AutoCalculate   In Excel, a software feature that sums the selected range of cells and displays the result in the Status bar.

AutoComplete   In Excel, a software feature that assists you in entering data into a worksheet by filling in letters from existing entries in the column as you type.

AutoFill   In Excel, a software feature that enables you to copy and extend a formula or data series automatically in a worksheet.

AutoFit   In Excel, a software feature that calculates the optimal row height or column width based on existing data in the worksheet.

AutoFormat   A software feature that applies professionally designed formatting styles to your documents.

AutoSum   A software feature that automatically inserts a formula for adding values from a surrounding row or column of cells.

bar chart   A chart that compares one data element to another data element using horizontal bars. Similar to a *column chart*.

cell   The intersection of a column and a row.

cell address   The location of a cell on a worksheet given by the intersection of a column and a row. Columns are labeled using letters. Rows are numbered. A cell address combines the column letter with the row number (for example, B9 or DF134.)

cell alignment   The positioning of data entered into a worksheet cell in relation to the cell borders.

cell pointer   The cursor on a worksheet that points to a cell. The cell pointer is moved using the arrow keys or the mouse.

cell range   One or more cells in a worksheet that together form a rectangle.

chart sheet   A sheet tab or page within a workbook file that is used to create, modify, and display a chart graphic.

Chart Wizard   A linear step progression of dialog boxes that leads you through creating a chart in Excel.

column chart   A chart that compares one data element with another data element and can show variations over a period of time.

document window   In Excel, each open *workbook* appears in its own document window. These windows may be sized and moved anywhere within the application window.

drag and drop   A software feature that allows you to copy and move information by dragging information from one location to another using the mouse.

embedded chart   A chart that is placed on the draw layer of a worksheet.

fill handle   The small black square that is located in the bottom right-hand corner of a cell or cell range. You use the fill handle to create a series or to copy cell information.

font(s)   All the characters of one size in a particular *typeface*; includes numbers, punctuation marks, and uppercase and lowercase letters.

footer(s)   Descriptive information (such as page number and date) that appears at the bottom of each page of a document.

Format Painter   A software feature that enables you to copy only the formatting attributes and styles from one location to another.

formula   A mathematical expression that typically defines the relationships among various cells in a worksheet or table.

Formula Palette   The dialog box, appearing beneath the Formula bar, that provides assistance for entering a function's *arguments* using the correct syntax.

functions   Built-in shortcuts that can be used in formulas to perform calculations.

gridlines   The lines on a worksheet that assist the user in lining up the cell pointer with a particular column letter or row number.

header(s)   Descriptive information (such as page number and data) that appears at the top of each page of a document.

HTML   An acronym for Hypertext Markup Language, which is the standardized markup language used in creating documents for display on the World Wide Web.

hyperlinks   In terms of Internet technologies, a text string or graphics that when clicked take you to another location, either within the same document or to a separate document stored on your computer, an intranet resource, or onto the Internet.

in-cell editing   In Excel, the feature that enables you to revise text labels, numbers, dates, and other entries directly within a cell. To activate in-cell editing, you double-click a cell.

Internet   A worldwide network of computer networks that are interconnected by standard telephone lines, fiber optics, and satellites.

intranet   A private local or wide area network that uses Internet protocols and technologies to share information within an institution or corporation.

line chart   A chart that plots trends or shows changes over a period of time.

macro virus   A malicious program that attaches itself to a document or template and performs instructions that may damage files on your computer.

margins   Space between the edge of the paper and the top, bottom, left, and right edges of the printed document.

mixed cell address   Cell reference in a worksheet that includes both *relative* and *absolute cell references*. For example, the address C$4 provides a "relative" column letter and an "absolute" row number.

Name box   The text box appearing at the left-hand side of the Formula bar that displays the current cell address and that enables you to navigate quickly to any cell location in the worksheet.

natural language formula   In Excel, a type of *formula* that allows you to use the column and row labels within a worksheet in building a mathematical expression.

Office Clipboard   A program, in Microsoft Office 2000, that allows you to copy and move information within or among Office 2000 applications. Unlike the Windows Clipboard, the Office Clipboard can store up to 12 items and then paste them all at once.

pie chart   A chart that shows the proportions of individual components compared to the whole.

Places bar   The strip of icon buttons appearing in the Open and Save As dialog boxes that allow you to display the most common areas for retrieving and storing files using a single mouse click.

range name   A name that is given to a range of cells in the worksheet. This name can then be used in formulas and functions to refer to the cell range.

Redo command   A command that makes it possible to reverse the effects of an Undo command.

relative cell address   Default cell reference in a worksheet that automatically adjusts when copied to other cells.

series   A sequence of numbers or dates that follows a mathematical or date pattern.

scatter plot chart   A chart that shows how one or more data elements relate to another data element. Also called *XY charts*.

syntax   The rules, structure, and order of *arguments* used in entering a formula or function.

template   A workbook or document that has been saved to a special file and location so that it may be used again and again as a model for creating new documents.

typeface(s)   The shape and appearance of characters. There are two categories of typefaces: serif and sans serif. Serif type (for example, Times Roman) is more decorative and, some say, easier to read than sans serif type (for example, Arial).

Undo command   A command that makes it possible to reverse up to the last 16 commands or actions performed.

Windows Clipboard   A program, in Windows, that allows you to copy and move information within an application or among applications. The Windows Clipboard temporarily stores the information in memory before you paste the data in a new location.

wizard   A program or process whereby a series of dialog boxes lead you step-by-step through performing a procedure.

workbook   The disk file that contains the *worksheets* and *chart sheets* that you create in Excel.

worksheet   A sheet tab or page within a workbook file that is used to create, modify, and display a worksheet grid of columns and rows.

World Wide Web   A visual interface to the Internet based on *hyperlinks*. Using Web browser software, you click on hyperlinks to navigate resources on the Internet.

XY charts   Charts that show how one or more data elements relate to another data element. Also called *scatter plot diagrams*.

Appendix: Microsoft Windows Quick Reference

Using the Mouse and Keyboard

Microsoft Windows provides a graphical environment for working in your application, such as Microsoft Word, Excel, Access, or Power-Point. As you work with Windows applications, you will find that there are often three different ways to perform the same command. The most common methods for performing commands include:

- Menu   Choose a command from the Menu bar or from a right-click menu.
- Mouse   Position the mouse pointer over a toolbar button and then click once.
- Keyboard   Press a keyboard shortcut (usually `CTRL` + *letter*).

Although you may use a Windows application with only a keyboard, much of a program's basic design relies on using a mouse. Regardless of whether your mouse has two or three buttons, you will use the left or primary mouse button for selecting screen objects and menu commands and the right or secondary mouse button for displaying right-click menus.

The most common mouse actions include:

- Point   Slide the mouse on your desk to position the tip of the mouse pointer over the desired object on the screen.
- Click   Press down and release the left mouse button quickly. Clicking is used to select a screen object, activate a toolbar command, and choose menu commands.
- Right-Click   Press down and release the right mouse button. Right-clicking the mouse pointer on a screen object displays a context-sensitive menu.
- Double-Click   Press down and release the mouse button twice in rapid succession. Double-clicking is used to select screen objects or to activate an embedded object for editing.
- Drag   Press down and hold the mouse button as you move the mouse pointer across the screen. When the mouse pointer reaches the desired location, release the mouse button. Dragging is used to select a group of screen objects and to copy or move data.

You may notice that the mouse pointer changes shape as you move it over different parts of the screen. Each mouse pointer shape has its own purpose and may provide you with important information. There are four primary mouse shapes that appear in Windows applications:

↖	arrow	Used to choose menu commands and click toolbars buttons.
⧗	hourglass	Informs you that the application is occupied and requests that you wait.
I	I-beam	Used to set the position of the insertion point and to modify and edit text.
☝	hand	Used to select hyperlinks in the Windows-based Help systems, in Microsoft Office documents, and on the Web.

Aside from being the primary input device for entering information, the keyboard offers shortcut methods for performing some common commands and procedures.

Starting Windows

Because Windows is an operating system, it is loaded into the computer's memory when you first turn on the computer. To start Windows, you must do the following:

1. Turn on the power switches to the computer and monitor. After a few seconds, the Windows desktop will appear. (*Note*: If you are attached to a network, a dialog box may appear asking you to enter your User name and Password. Enter this information now or ask your instructor for further instructions.)
2. A Welcome dialog box may appear providing information about the operating system's major features. If the Welcome dialog box appears on your screen:
   CLICK: Close button (⊠) in the top right-hand corner of the Welcome window
3. If additional windows appear open on your desktop:
   CLICK: Close button (⊠) in the top right-hand corner of each window

EXCEL

Parts of a Dialog Box

A dialog box is a common mechanism in Windows applications for collecting information before processing a command. In a dialog box, you indicate the options you want to use and then click the OK button when you're finished. Dialog boxes are also used to display messages or to ask for the confirmation of commands. The following shows an example of the Print dialog box, which is similar across Windows applications.

Print dialog box

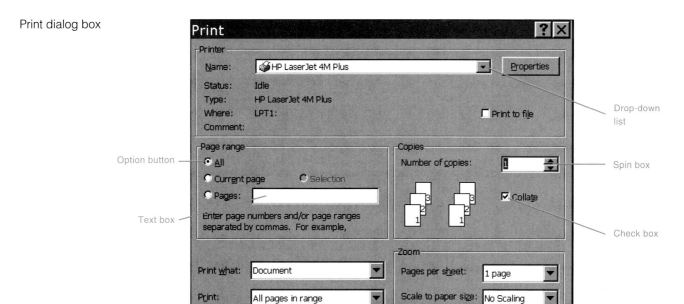

A dialog box uses several types of controls or components for collecting information. We describe the most common components in the following table.

Dialog box components

Name	Example	Action
Check box	☑ Always ☐ Never	Click an option to turn it on or off. The option is turned on when an "✔" appears in the box.
Command button	OK Cancel	Click a command button to execute an action. Click OK to accept your selections or click Cancel to exit the dialog box.

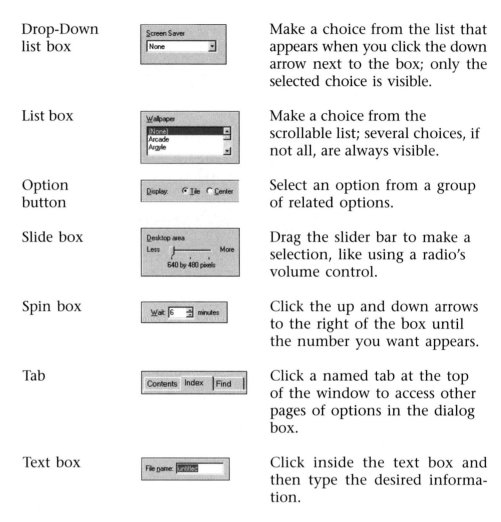

Drop-Down list box	Make a choice from the list that appears when you click the down arrow next to the box; only the selected choice is visible.
List box	Make a choice from the scrollable list; several choices, if not all, are always visible.
Option button	Select an option from a group of related options.
Slide box	Drag the slider bar to make a selection, like using a radio's volume control.
Spin box	Click the up and down arrows to the right of the box until the number you want appears.
Tab	Click a named tab at the top of the window to access other pages of options in the dialog box.
Text box	Click inside the text box and then type the desired information.

Most dialog boxes provide a question mark icon ([?]) near the right side of the Title bar. If you have a question about an item in the dialog box, click the question mark and then click the item to display a pop-up help window. To remove the help window, click on it once.

Getting Help

Windows applications, such as Microsoft Office 2000 applications, provide a comprehensive library of online documentation. This section describes these help features and how to find more detailed information.

Obtaining Context-Sensitive Help

In Windows applications, you can often retrieve context-sensitive help for menu options, toolbar buttons, and dialog box items. *Context-sensitive help* refers to a program's ability to present helpful information reflecting your current position in the program. The help information is presented concisely in a small pop-up window that you can remove with the click of the mouse. This type of help lets you access information quickly and then continue working without interruption. The following table describes some methods for accessing context-sensitive help while working in Windows applications.

Displaying context-sensitive
Help information

To display...	*Do this...*
A description of a dialog box item	Click the question mark button ([?]) in a dialog box's Title bar and then click an item in the dialog box. Alternatively, you can often right-click a dialog box item and then choose the What's This? command from the shortcut menu.
A description of a menu command	Choose the Help, What's This? command from the menu and then choose a command using the question mark mouse pointer. Rather than executing the command, a helpful description of the command appears in a pop-up window.
A description of a toolbar button	Point to a toolbar button to display a pop-up label called a ToolTip.

Getting Help in Office 2000

Getting Help from the Office Assistant

In Office 2000 applications, the Office Assistant is your personal computer guru and is available by default when your application is first installed. When you need to perform a task that you're unsure of, simply click the Assistant character and then type a phrase such as "How do I obtain help" in the Assistant balloon. The Assistant analyzes your request and provides a resource list of suggested topics, as shown to the right. Simply click a topic to obtain additional information.

The Assistant also watches your keystrokes and mouse clicks as you work and offers suggestions and shortcuts to make you more productive and efficient. If you find the Office Assistant to be distracting, you can turn it off by choosing "Hide the Office Assistant" from the Help menu. To redisplay it, simply choose "Microsoft *Application* Help" or "Show the Office Assistant" from the Help menu.

Getting Help from the Help Window

You may prefer to obtain a complete topical listing of your application's Help system. To do this, you must first disable the Office Assistant by clicking the Options button in the Assistant balloon, clearing the *Use the Office Assistant* check box, and then pressing (ENTER). Once the Office Assistant is disabled, simply choose "Microsoft *Application* Help" from the Help menu to display the Help window. If the *Contents*, *Answer Wizard*, and *Index* tabs don't appear, click Show (⧉) in the window's toolbar.

The Help window, shown below, provides three different tools, each on its own tab, to help you find the information you need quickly and easily. You can read the Help information you find onscreen or print it out for later reference by clicking the Print button (🖨) in the window's toolbar. To close the Help window, click its Close button (☒).

Example Help window

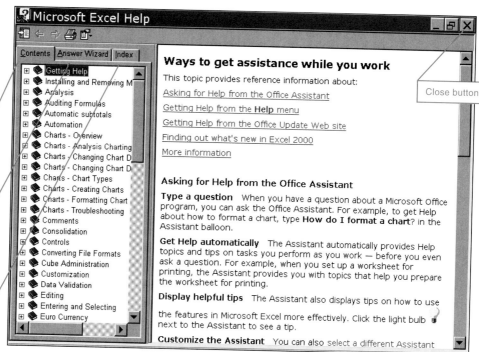

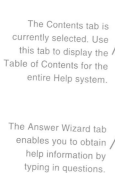

The Contents tab is currently selected. Use this tab to display the Table of Contents for the entire Help system.

The Answer Wizard tab enables you to obtain help information by typing in questions.

The Index tab displays enables you to display topics by selecting keywords or typing in words and phrases.

Getting Help from the Office Update Web Site

Microsoft's Office Update Web site provides additional technical support and product enhancements. You can access this site from any Office application by choosing "Office on the Web" from the Help menu.

Index

ABS key (absolute key), EX-157
Absolute cell addresses, EX-157, EX-179
Accept labels in formulas check box, EX-160
Active sheet tab, EX-9
Adaptive menus, disabling, EX-10
Adding values (SUM), EX-163–EX-164
Addition, EX-19
Align Left button, EX-12, EX-108
Alignment formatting options, EX-108
Alignment of cells, EX-107–EX-109, EX-133
Alignment tab, EX-133
Align Right button, EX-12, EX-108
Answer Wizard tab, AP-204–AP-205
Application window components, EX-8, EX-9
Arguments defined, EX-161
Arrow mouse pointer, AP-200
As object in option button, EX-175
Assistant character, EX-8, AP-204
   hiding, EX-10
   location, EX-9
AutoCalculate feature, EX-59–EX-60, EX-83
AutoComplete feature
   pick lists, EX-57–EX-58
   turning off, EX-56
   word acceptance, EX-57
AutoFill feature, EX-70–EX-72
AutoFit feature, EX-74–EX-76
AutoFormat dialog box, EX-120
AutoFormat feature, EX-112, EX-119–EX-120, EX-134
Automatic updating, EX-20
AutoSum button, EX-12, EX-59, EX-83, EX-163
AutoSum feature, EX-59
AVERAGE function, EX-164, EX-180
Averages, calculating, EX-164, EX-180

Back button, EX-31
Backspace key, EX-21
Bar charts, EX-171
Bold button, EX-12, EX-73, EX-102–EX-103
Boldface, EX-102
Borders, EX-110–EX-112, EX-134
Borders button, EX-12, EX-110
Buttons
   Align Left, EX-12, EX-108
   Align Right, EX-12, EX-108
   AutoSum, EX-12, EX-59, EX-83, EX-163
   Back, EX-31
   Bold, EX-12, EX-73, EX-102–EX-103
   Borders, EX-12, EX-110
   Cancel, EX-15
   Center, EX-12, EX-108
   ... EX-173

Buttons—*Cont.*
   Custom Footer, EX-128
   Custom Header, EX-128
   Cut, EX-12, EX-83
   Decrease Decimal, EX-12, EX-105, EX-133
   Decrease Indent, EX-12
   Delete, EX-31
   Desktop, EX-31
   Edit Formula, EX-167–EX-168
   E-Mail, EX-12
   Enter, EX-15
   Favorites, EX-31
   Fill Color, EX-12, EX-110–EX-111
   Font Color, EX-12, EX-102, EX-111
   Format Painter, EX-12, EX-112, EX-114, EX-134
   Help, EX-12
   History, EX-31
   Increase Decimal, EX-12, EX-105, EX-106, EX-133
   Increase Indent, EX-12
   Insert Hyperlink, EX-12
   Italic, EX-12, EX-102–EX-103
   Map, EX-12
   Maximize, EX-8
   Merge and Center, EX-12, EX-108
   Minimize, EX-8
   My Documents, EX-31
   New, EX-12, EX-21, EX-28, EX-35, EX-70
   Open, EX-12, EX-32, EX-35
   Other Tools, EX-31
   Paste, EX-12, EX-65, EX-83
   Paste All button, EX-67
   Paste Function, EX-12, EX-161
   Percent Style, EX-12, EX-105
   Preview, EX-134
   Print, EX-12, EX-122, EX-134, EX-180
   Print Preview, EX-12, EX-122, EX-177, EX-180
   Question mark, AP-203
   Redo, EX-12, EX-25, EX-36
   Restore, EX-8
   Save, EX-12, EX-30, EX-35
   Search the Web, EX-31
   Select All, EX-77
   Show, AP-204
   Sort Ascending, EX-12
   Sort Descending, EX-12
   Spelling, EX-12
   Start, EX-7, EX-35
   Top and Double Bottom Border, EX-111
   Underline, EX-12, EX-102
   Undo, EX-12, EX-25, EX-36
   Up One Level, EX-31
   Views, EX-31, EX-33
   Web Folders, EX-31, EX-125
   Zoom command, EX-177

C

CALC key, EX-169, EX-179
Calculations using AutoCalculate and AutoSum, EX-59, EX-83
Cancel button, EX-15
Cascading menus, EX-7
Category list box, EX-106, EX-107
   ... text box, EX-174

Cell addresses—*Cont.*
   displaying, EX-13
   dollar signs in, EX-157
   mixed, EX-157, EX-179
   moving to, EX-13
   relative, EX-157, EX-179
Cell pointer
   location, EX-9
   moving, EX-13–EX-15
Cell ranges
   defined, EX-53, EX-151
   deleting, EX-61–EX-63, EX-83
   formulas in, EX-53, EX-74, EX-84
   inserting, EX-61–EX-63, EX-83
   minimum and maximum values in, EX-167–EX-168, EX-180
   naming, EX-151–EX-156, EX-179
   selecting, EX-54–EX-56
Cell references, EX-179
Cells
   aligning, EX-107–EX-109, EX-133
   copying contents of, EX-72
   dashed lines around, EX-19
   data entry, EX-12–EX-21
   defined, EX-5
   deleting, EX-61–EX-63, EX-83
   editing, EX-21–EX-26, EX-36
   erasing, EX-23–EX-24, EX-36
   inserting, EX-61–EX-63, EX-83
   location, EX-9
   merging, EX-107–EX-109, EX-133
Center button, EX-12, EX-108
Character formatting, EX-102–EX-104
Charts
   bar, EX-171
   column, EX-171
   creating, EX-170–EX-176, EX-180
   dragging, EX-175
   dynamically linked to information, EX-176
   embedded, EX-170, EX-173
   line, EX-170
   pie, EX-171–EX-172
   previewing, EX-177–EX-178, EX-180
   printing, EX-173, EX-177–EX-178, EX-180
   scatter plot, EX-172
   sizing, EX-175
   XY, EX-172
Chart sheets
   defined, EX-5–EX-6
   format, EX-6
   storage, EX-6
Chart Wizard, EX-173–EX-176, EX-180
Chart Wizard button, EX-12, EX-173, EX-180
Check boxes, AP-201
Chevrons, EX-9, EX-11
Clear Clipboard button, EX-66–EX-67, EX-84
Click defined, AP-199
Clipboards
   difference between, EX-65
   keyboard shortcuts for, EX-64
   menu commands for, EX-64
   toolbar buttons for, EX-64
Close button, EX-7, EX-8, EX-30, EX-35
Closing, EX-7
Colon (:), EX-53
Color drop-down list box, EX-104
   ... 13

Column charts, EX-171
Column headings
   date values, EX-17
   printing, EX-131
   text labels, EX-15–EX-16, EX-159–EX-160
Columns
   changing widths, EX-74–EX-76, EX-84
   checking for data in, EX-79
   deleting, EX-78–EX-80, EX-84
   hiding, EX-81–EX-82, EX-84
   inserting, EX-78–EX-80, EX-84
   right-click menu for, EX-80
   unhiding, EX-81–EX-82, EX-84
Column Width dialog box, EX-75
Command buttons, AP-201
Commands
   context-sensitive, EX-10
   dimmed, EX-9
   followed by an ellipsis, EX-9
   reversible, EX-26
Commas, EX-18, EX-104
Comma Style button, EX-12, EX-105
Comments added to a screen, EX-106–EX-107
Computer-based presentations, EX-173
Contents tab, AP-204–AP-205
Context-sensitive commands, EX-10
Context-sensitive menus, EX-10
Copy button, EX-12, EX-65, EX-83, EX-117, EX-134
Copy command, EX-65
Copying
   and cell addresses, EX-157–EX-158
   of data, EX-63–EX-74, EX-83
   of formatting, EX-113–EX-115, EX-134
   of formulas, EX-73, EX-84
   using drag and drop, EX-68–EX-70, EX-83–EX-84
COUNT function, EX-166, EX-180
Create Name dialog box, EX-153
Create New Folder button, EX-31, EX-32, EX-35
Currency Style button, EX-12, EX-105, EX-106
Custom Footer button, EX-128
Custom Header button, EX-128
Custom Header dialog box, EX-129
Customize dialog box, EX-11
Cut button, EX-12, EX-83
Cut command, EX-64

Dashed lines
   around cells, EX-19
   in clipboard maneuvers, EX-66
Data
   in columns, EX-79
   copying, EX-63–EX-74, EX-83
   inserting, EX-64
   moving, EX-63–EX-74, EX-83
Database functions, EX-162
Data comparison charts, EX-171
Data entry, EX-12–EX-21
   dates, EX-16–EX-17, EX-36
   errors, EX-21
   formulas, EX-19–EX-21, EX-36
   numbers, EX-18, EX-36
   text, EX-15–EX-16
   using AutoComplete, EX-56–EX-58, EX-83
Data files, EX-31

Date functions, EX-180
Dates
    calculating, EX-169–EX-170
    entering, EX-16–EX-17, EX-36
    formatting, EX-104–EX-107
Date & Time functions, EX-162
Date values
    arithmetic calculations, EX-16–
        EX-17
    as column headings, EX-17
Decimal places, EX-104
    increasing and decreasing, EX-12,
        EX-105, EX-106, EX-133
Decimal places text box, EX-106
Decrease Decimal button, EX-12,
    EX-105, EX-133
Decrease Indent button, EX-12
Define Name dialog box, EX-155
Delete button, EX-31
Delete key, EX-23, EX-36
Depreciation schedules, EX-162
Desktop button, EX-31
Dialog box components, AP-201–
    AP-202
Dialog box item descriptions, AP-203
Dimmed commands, EX-9
Display window, EX-8
Division, EX-19
Docked toolbars, EX-12
Document window components,
    EX-8
Dollar signs, EX-18, EX-104
    in cell addresses, EX-157
Double-Click defined, AP-199
Drag and drop, EX-63, EX-68–EX-70,
    EX-83–EX-84
Drag defined, AP-199
Drawing button, EX-12
Drop-down lists, AP-201–AP-202

Edit, Clear command, EX-23–EX-24
Edit, Fill commands, EX-72
Edit, Paste Special command,
    EX-112, EX-117–EX-118
Edit Formula button, EX-167–
    EX-168
Editing cells, EX-21–EX-26, EX-36
Edit key, EX-21, EX-23, EX-36
Ellipsis, EX-9
E-Mail button, EX-12
Enable AutoComplete for cell values
    check box, EX-56
Enable Micros command, EX-29
Enter button, EX-15
Enter key, EX-15
Equal sign (=), EX-19, EX-159
Erasing cells, EX-23–EX-24, EX-36
Error-checking, EX-162
Esc key, EX-15
Excel earlier versions, EX-34–EX-35
Exclamation point (!), EX-151
Exiting, EX-7–EX-8, EX-35
Explorer, EX-32

Favorites button, EX-31
File, Close command, EX-30
File, New command, EX-28
File, Open command, EX-32
File, Page Setup command, EX-126,
    EX-134
File, Save command, EX-30–EX-32
File management, EX-27–EX-34
File name text box, EX-31
Files
    naming, EX-27
    from other programs, EX-34–EX-35
Files of type drop-down list box,
    EX-34, EX-35
Fill Color button, EX-12, EX-110–
    EX-111

Fill handles
    creating a series with, EX-84
    defined, EX-70
Financial functions, EX-162
Floating toolbars, EX-12
Fly-out menus, EX-7
Folders
    creating, EX-32, EX-35
    default, EX-31
    management, EX-32
    Web, EX-31, EX-125
Font Color button, EX-12, EX-102,
    EX-111
Font list box, EX-12, EX-102–
    EX-104
Fonts, EX-102
    color for, EX-12, EX-102, EX-111
Font Size list box, EX-12, EX-102–
    EX-104
Font sizes
    adjusting, EX-102
    applying, EX-133
Font styles, EX-102
    applying, EX-133
Footers, EX-126
    inserting, EX-128–EX-130
    printing, EX-135
Format Cells dialog box
    Alignment tab, EX-109, EX-133
    Font tab, EX-104
    Number tab, EX-106
Format Painter button, EX-12,
    EX-112, EX-114, EX-134
Format Painter feature, EX-113–
    EX-115
Formatting
    applying, EX-112–EX-120
    of characters, EX-102–EX-104
    clearing, EX-134
    copying, EX-113–EX-115, EX-134
    of dates, EX-104–EX-107
    of fonts, EX-102–EX-104
    keyboard shortcuts, EX-104
    of numbers, EX-18, EX-104–
        EX-107, EX-133
    removing, EX-112, EX-116–EX-120
Formatting toolbar
    components, EX-12
    customizing, EX-11, EX-35
    location, EX-9
    uses, EX-12
Formula bar
    editing in, EX-21, EX-36
    location, EX-8–EX-9
Formula Palette, EX-167–EX-168,
    EX-180
    using, EX-180
Formulas
    copying, EX-73, EX-84
    defined, EX-19
    duplicating, EX-63
    entering, EX-19–EX-21, EX-36
    extending across a row, EX-72
    extending down a column, EX-72
    natural language, EX-159–EX-160
    recalculating, EX-179
    using references in, EX-157–
        EX-158
    using row and column labels,
        EX-159–EX-160
Functions
    built-in, EX-161
    categories of, EX-162
    inserting, EX-180
    using, EX-83, EX-161–EX-162,
        EX-167–EX-168, EX-180

GoTo key, EX-13
Gridlines, EX-126
    printing, EX-131
    reestablishing, EX-112
    removing, EX-110
Gridlines check box, EX-132

Hand mouse pointer, AP-200
Headers, EX-126
    inserting, EX-128–EX-130
    printing, EX-135
Headings, range names from,
    EX-152, EX-153
Help
    context-sensitive, AP-203
    from Help windows, AP-204
    from Office Assistant, AP-204
    from Office Update Web Site,
        AP-205
Help, What's This? AP-203
Help button, EX-12
Help windows, AP-205
    removing, AP-202
    using, AP-204
History button, EX-31
Horizontal drop-down list box, EX-109
Horizontal scroll box, EX-9
Hourglass mouse pointer, AP-200
HTML (Hypertext Markup Language),
    EX-124
Hyperlinks defined, EX-121

I-beam mouse pointer, AP-200, EX-23
IF statements, EX-162
Inactive sheet tab, EX-9
In-cell editing, EX-21–EX-23, EX-36
Increase Decimal button, EX-12,
    EX-105, EX-106, EX-133
Increase Indent button, EX-12
Index tab, AP-204–AP-205
Information functions, EX-162
Insert Hyperlink button, EX-12
Insertion point, flashing, EX-21
Internet defined, EX-121
Intranet defined, EX-121
Inventory worksheet, EX-22
Invoice template icon, EX-29
Italic, EX-102
Italic button, EX-12, EX-102–
    EX-103

Keyboard shortcuts, AP-199
    to apply formatting, EX-104
    for copying data, EX-64
    for inserting data, EX-64
    for moving data, EX-64
    to undo, EX-26, EX-36
    worksheet navigation, EX-13–
        EX-15, EX-36, EX-55

Landscape orientation, EX-127,
    EX-134
Line charts, EX-170
List boxes, AP-202
Loading, EX-7–EX-8, EX-35
Loan payments, EX-162
Logical functions, EX-162
Look in drop-down list box, EX-33
Lookup & Reference functions,
    EX-162
Lotus, EX-34

Macro virus defined, EX-29
Map button, EX-12
Margins, EX-126, EX-134
Mathematical operators, EX-19
Math & Trig functions, EX-162
MAX functions, EX-167–EX-168,
    EX-180

Maximize button, EX-8
McGraw-Hill Information
    Technology Web site, EX-x
Menu bar, AP-199
    contents, EX-9
    location, EX-8–EX-9
Menu commands
    for copying data, EX-64
    descriptions, AP-203
    dimmed, EX-9
    executing, EX-9
    followed by an ellipsis, EX-9
    for inserting data, EX-64
    for moving data, EX-64
Menus
    adaptive, EX-10
    cascading, EX-7
    chevrons on, EX-9, EX-11
    context-sensitive, EX-10
    customizing, EX-10–EX-12,
        EX-35
    fly-out, EX-7
    pop-up, EX-7
    pull-down, EX-9
    right-click, EX-10, EX-80
*Menus show recently used commands
    first* check box, EX-10
Merge and Center button, EX-12,
    EX-108
Merge cells check box, EX-109,
    EX-133
Merging cells, EX-107–EX-109
Microsoft *Application* Help, AP-204
MIN functions, EX-167–EX-168,
    EX-180
Minimize button, EX-8
Mixed cell addresses, EX-157,
    EX-179
Mouse, AP-199
Mouse actions, AP-199
Mouse pointer
    arrow, AP-200
    hand, AP-200
    hourglass, AP-200
    I-beam, EX-23, AP-200
Move bar, dragging, EX-12
Move selection after Enter check box,
    EX-16
Moving data
    using clipboards, EX-63–EX-74,
        EX-83
    using drag and drop, EX-68–EX-70,
        EX-83–EX-84
Moving toolbars, EX-12
Multiplication, EX-19
My Documents button, EX-31

Name box, EX-13, EX-152
    location, EX-8–EX-9
Names in workbook list box, EX-156
Naming. see also Range names
    of cell ranges, EX-151–EX-156,
        EX-179
    of workbook files, EX-27
    of workbooks, EX-32, EX-37
Natural language formulas,
    EX-159–EX-160
Negative numbers list box, EX-106
New button, EX-12, EX-21, EX-28,
    EX-35, EX-70
New dialog box
    General tab, EX-28
    Spreadsheet solutions tab, EX-28,
        EX-35
New Folder dialog box, EX-32
Notes added to a screen, EX-106–EX-107
NOW function, EX-169–EX-170,
    EX-180
Numbers
    entering, EX-18, EX-36
    formatting, EX-104–EX-107,
        EX-133
    raw versus formatted, EX-18

Microsoft Excel 2000

Office Assistant
  help from, AP-204
  icon location, EX-9
Office Assistant character, EX-8–EX-9
  hiding, EX-10
Office Clipboard
  clearing, EX-84
  difference from Windows Clipboard, EX-65
  displaying contents, EX-64, EX-66, EX-84
  pasting contents, EX-66
  toolbar for, EX-66
  using, EX-63–EX-68
Office Update Web Site, AP-205
Open button, EX-12, EX-32, EX-37
Open dialog box, EX-32, EX-33
Open Office Document command, EX-32
Option buttons, AP-201–AP-202
Options dialog box
  Calculation tab, EX-160
  Edit tab, EX-16
Other Tools button, EX-31

Page design, EX-102
Page Setup dialog box, EX-126
  Header/Footer tab, EX-137
  Page tab, EX-128
  Sheet tab, EX-132
Paper size, EX-127
Password, AP-200
Paste All button, EX-67
Paste button, EX-12, EX-65, EX-83
Paste Function button, EX-12, EX-161
Paste Function dialog box, EX-161, EX-180
Paste Special command, EX-112, EX-117–EX-118
Paste Special dialog box, EX-118
Patterns, EX-110–EX-112, EX-134
Percentage symbols, EX-18, EX-104
Percent Style button, EX-12, EX-105
Pick lists from AutoComplete, EX-57–EX-58
Pie charts, EX-171–EX-172
Places bar, EX-31, EX-125
Point defined, AP-199
Pointing method, EX-19
Point size, EX-77
Pop-up menus, EX-7
Portrait orientation, EX-127, EX-134
Pound symbol (#), EX-75
Precedence, rules of, EX-19
Present and future values, EX-162
Presentations, computer-based, EX-173
Preview button, EX-134
Previewing
  of charts, EX-177–EX-178, EX-180
  of printing, EX-122–EX-124, EX-134
  of Web pages, EX-125–EX-126
Print button, EX-12, EX-122, EX-134, EX-180
Print dialog box, EX-124, EX-130, AP-201
Printing, EX-121, EX-122–EX-124, EX-134
  of charts, EX-173, EX-177–EX-178
  customizing options, EX-126–EX-132
  footers, EX-137
  headers, EX-137
  previewing, EX-122–EX-124, EX-134
  screen contents, EX-137
  of specified areas, EX-131, EX-134
Print orientation, EX-127, EX-134
Print Preview button, EX-12, EX-122, EX-177, EX-180
Print scale, EX-127
Pull-down menus, EX-9

Quattro Pro, EX-34
Question mark button, AP-203
Question mark icon, AP-202

Range names
  creating from labels, EX-179
  defined, EX-151
  deleting, EX-179
  from headings, EX-152, EX-153
  modifying, EX-179
  pasting, EX-155, EX-179
  removing, EX-156
  used for navigation, EX-153
Rates of return, EX-162
Redo button, EX-12, EX-25, EX-36
Redo command, EX-25–EX-26
Refer to text box, EX-156
Relative cell addresses, EX-157, EX-179
Restore button, EX-8
Right-Click defined, AP-199
Right-click menus, EX-80
  removing, EX-10
Rocky, EX-8
  hiding, EX-10
Row and column headings check box EX-132
Row headings
  printing, EX-131
  text labels, EX-15–EX-16, EX-159–EX-160
Row height text box, EX-78
Rows
  changing heights, EX-77–EX-78, EX-84
  deleting, EX-78–EX-80, EX-84
  hiding, EX-81–EX-82, EX-84
  inserting, EX-78–EX-80, EX-84
  unhiding, EX-81–EX-82, EX-84
Rules of precedence, EX-19

Save As command, EX-32
Save As dialog box, EX-30–EX-31, EX-35, EX-125
Save as type drop-down list box, EX-34, EX-125
Save button, EX-12, EX-30, EX-35
Save in drop-down list box, EX-31, EX-125
Saving
  frequency for, EX-27
  to hard drive, EX-31
  as Web page, EX-124–EX-125, EX-135
  of workbooks, EX-30–EX-32, EX-35
Scatter plot diagrams, EX-172
Scroll bars, EX-8
Scroll boxes, EX-9
Scroll Tip, EX-14
Search the Web button, EX-31
Select All button, EX-77
Selection handles, EX-176
Series
  creating, EX-70–EX-72, EX-84
  defined, EX-70
Shading, EX-110–EX-112, EX-134
Sheet tabs, EX-8
Shift cells down option button, EX-61
Shift cells right option button, EX-61
Show button, AP-204
Size list box, EX-104
Sizing handles, EX-176
Slide boxes, AP-202
Slide shows, EX-173
Social Security numbers, EX-18
Sort Ascending button, EX-12
Sort Descending button, EX-12
Spelling button, EX-12

Spin boxes, AP-201–AP-202
Spreadsheet software defined, EX-5
Standard and Formatting toolbars share one row check box, EX-11
Standard deviation, EX-162
Standard toolbar
  components, EX-12
  customizing, EX-11, EX-35
  location, EX-9
  uses, EX-12
Start, Documents command, EX-32
Start button, EX-7, EX-35
Starting Windows, AP-200
Start menu, EX-7
Statistical functions, EX-162
Statistical measures, EX-162
Status bar location, EX-8, EX-9
Student data files
  default folder, EX-31
  location, EX-27
Subtraction, EX-19
SUM function, EX-83, EX-163, EX-180
Syntax defined, EX-161

Tab key, EX-174
Table format list box, EX-119
Table formats predefined, EX-119–EX-120, EX-134
Tabs, AP-202
Tab Scrolling arrows, EX-8–EX-9
Tab Split box, EX-8–EX-9
Telephone numbers, EX-18
Templates
  custom, EX-28
  defined, EX-28
  viewing, EX-28
  for workbooks, EX-35
Text boxes, AP-201–AP-202
  moving through, EX-174
Text functions, EX-162
Text labels
  entering, EX-15–EX-16, EX-36
  for formulas, EX-159–EX-160
  range names created from, EX-179
Title bar icons, EX-8
Title bar location, EX-9
TODAY function, EX-169–EX-170, EX-180
Toolbar buttons
  for copying data, EX-64
  descriptions, AP-203
  for inserting data, EX-64
  for moving data, EX-64
Toolbars
  customizing, EX-10–EX-12, EX-35
  docked, EX-12
  floating, EX-12
  location, EX-8–EX-9
  moving, EX-12
Tools menu, EX-11
ToolTips, EX-66, AP-203
Top and Double Bottom Border button, EX-111
Trends, charts for, EX-170
Trigonometric calculations, EX-162
Troubleshooting, EX-162
Typefaces, EX-102
  applying, EX-133
  selecting, EX-103
Type list box, EX-107

Underline button, EX-12, EX-102
Undo button, EX-12, EX-25, EX-36
Undocked toolbars, EX-12
Undo command, EX-25–EX-26
Up One Level button, EX-31
User name, AP-200
Use 1000 Separator (,) check box, EX-106
Use the Office Assistant check box, AP-204

Values
  adding, EX-163–EX-164
  analyzing, EX-167–EX-168
  counting, EX-166, EX-180
Value (Y) axis text box, EX-174
Variance, EX-162
Vertical scroll bar, dragging, EX-14
Vertical scrollbox, EX-9
Views button, EX-31, EX-33
Virus defined, EX-29

Warning dialog boxes, EX-29
Web Folders button, EX-31, EX-125
Web page previews, EX-125–EX-126
Web publishing, EX-121, EX-124–EX-126
Web sites
  McGraw-Hill Information Technology, EX-27
  Office Update, AP-205
Welcome dialog box, AP-200
Windows Clipboard
  difference from Office Clipboard, EX-65
  using, EX-63–EX-68
Windows Explorer, EX-32
Windows icons location, EX-8–EX-9
Windows Start menu, EX-7
Wizards
  answer, AP-204–AP-205
  for charts, EX-12, EX-173–EX-176, EX-180
  defined, EX-28
Workbook files naming, EX-27
Workbooks
  closing, EX-30–EX-32, EX-35
  creating, EX-28–EX-29, EX-35
  defined, EX-6
  opening, EX-32–EX-34, EX-35
  relationship to worksheets, EX-151
  renaming, EX-32, EX-35
  saving, EX-30–EX-32, EX-35
  templates for, EX-35
Worksheets
  components, EX-5
  creating, EX-12–EX-21
  defined, EX-5
  format, EX-6
  navigation keystrokes, EX-13–EX-15, EX-36
  relationship to workbooks, EX-151
  saving as a Web page, EX-124–EX-125, EX-135
  storage, EX-6
  viewing as a Web page, EX-124–EX-126, EX-134
World Wide Web defined, EX-121

XY charts, EX-172

Zip codes, EX-18
Zoom command button, EX-177
Zooming in and out, EX-123